Susan's Magic

Susan's Magic

by Nan Hayden Agle

drawings by Charles Robinson

THE SEABURY PRESS · NEW YORK

Text copyright © 1973 by Nan Hayden Agle
Illustrations copyright © 1973 by The Seabury Press
Designed by Paula Wiener
Printed in the United States of America

Library of Congress Cataloging in Publication Data

Agle, Nan Hayden
    Susan's magic.

SUMMARY: Aided by a cat, Susan uses her intuition
to help an old lady save her faltering antique shop.
    1. Robinson, Charles, 1931 illus.
    2. Title
PZ7.A2678Su   (Fic)   737124
ISBN: 0-8164-3108-6

U. S. 1776518

FOR NANCY DAVIS CECIL

Thanks to: Jim Giblin and Jim Murphy

Contents

1. A Secret Mission, 13
2. The Flea Market, 19
3. The White Elephant, 27
4. The Gaffney Debt, 32
5. The Birthday Present, 40
6. Stanley Trunko, 47
7. Sereena, 56
8. Something Has to Be Done, 64
9. Gaffney's Antique Shop, 72
10. Gone But Not Forgotten, 81
11. Sereena Salescat, 90
12. Thick as Thieves, 102
13. The Cat's Place, 113
14. The Bargain, 121
15. A Magic Wand, 131

Susan's Magic

1

A Secret Mission

THE FRONT DOOR of the Prescott house, number 5 Bird Lane, opened and Susan stepped out, saying over her shoulder, "I'm leaving now, Mother. See you later."

Before Susan reached the gate, Mrs. Prescott called from the porch, "I wish you'd be sensible and let me drive you to the village."

"Not today." Susan stopped, looked back, and added, "I told you over and over again that this was a secret mission and you said I could go alone. Remember, Mother? You said so yesterday."

"I suppose I did," Mother answered anxiously. "Well, take your time, be careful crossing the street, don't speak to any strangers, and come home as soon as you've tended to your mysterious errand."

"Okay, and don't worry about me. After all, people can't let other people take them everywhere forever."

"I guess not," Mother said.

Susan spun around on her heel, then walked through the gate and down the hill—a short girl in a short skirt, long red pocketbook over her shoulder. At Falls Road she turned left and ran past Antique Row as fast as she could run. She didn't mind the two big shops but she hated the narrow one between them.

It was a spooky house, old shingles falling off, chimney leaning, the sign—*Gaffney's Antiques*—hanging by one nail, the letters faded so you could hardly see them. Although Susan didn't actually look toward the pinched little house, didn't dare to, she could feel old Mrs. Gaffney watching her from the upstairs window. She slept up there and ate in the kitchen behind the shop, so people said.

That wasn't all they said, either. They said she used to tell fortunes, read palms and that sort of thing, until the police or somebody made her stop. The reason they did, so Susan heard, was because she told a woman she better drive carefully or she'd have an accident, and right away that woman ran into a pole, broke her collar bone, and blamed it on Mrs. Gaffney.

Because of that and a couple of other things, some people said Mrs. Gaffney was a witch. Not Mother. Mother said there wasn't any such thing as a witch. You couldn't count on that, though, because Mother said Susan's magic was purely imagination too—and it wasn't. Susan could tell about things and make them turn out the way she wanted them to. Not always, but enough times to be on the side of magic.

Maybe Mother was right about Mrs. Gaffney, maybe she wasn't. For sure the old woman looked like a witch — tall, shoulders bent, hollow-eyed, gray hair going in all directions. Just the thought of her gave Susan the shudders, and as they were practically neighbors she had to think about her almost every day.

As soon as she was safely past Antique Row Susan slowed down to a swift walk and in no time was crossing the bridge, skirt swinging. On the other side, at the corner by the grocery store, she bumped into Joyce Gibbs who was carrying a large sofa pillow in her arms, a green monster with a waterfall painted on one side, gold braid around the edge.

Joyce was in the sixth grade at Mt. Washington Elementary School. Susan, a fourth grader, didn't like her much; Joyce was a showoff and too bossy besides. She liked her some, though. They both played dodgeball, and both of their parents were divorced which made sort of a bond between them.

Not much of a bond, though, as their situations were not a bit alike. Joyce's father lived in town and she saw him nearly every week. He spoiled her something terrible, gave her much too much for her own good, so Mother said. Susan's father didn't spoil her. He lived in St. Louis, Missouri, and almost never came to Baltimore.

"Hi, Joyce."

"Hi, Susan. Where are you going all by yourself? I've never seen you out except with your mother leading you around. How come she let you off the leash at last? Is it your birthday?"

"No, but tomorrow is my mother's birthday. I'm on a shopping trip now to buy her a surprise present. It's my first time on my own."

"I was on my own when I was five," boasted Joyce. "Until you are, you don't know who you are."

"I know who I am—Susan Prescott, that's who."

"I don't mean that. I mean what kind of a person you are."

"You mean success or failure, dependent or independent, a mixer or a loner, a giver or a taker, a—?"

"Yes, yes, Susan. You get the point."

"Well, right now I'm independent. I'm going where I want to go, I'm going to buy what I want to buy, and I'm going to pay for it with my own money. Listen."

Susan shook the red pocketbook and the jingle was impressive.

"How much do you have?" Joyce asked. "I get two dollars a week allowance from my mother and twice that from my father."

"Fifty cents in pennies earned by me," stated Susan

proudly, ignoring Joyce's financial report. "I washed dishes for my brother Mike when it was his turn to. Now I'm going to spend it all on a real nice present at the drugstore or the Boutique or the flower shop."

"There is only *one* place to shop today," Joyce said, her green eyes peering over the top of the green pillow, "the Flea Market at St. John's Church. It's really great. I've just come from there and I'm going back right after my music lesson."

"Flea Market?" Susan frowned.

"For your information, stupid, a flea market is nothing more than a bunch of white elephant tables."

"White elephant?"

"If you don't know what a white elephant is you'd better go back to kindergarten and start over. It's something somebody doesn't want that somebody else might. This is one." Joyce thrust the green pillow straight out in front of her, nearly poking Susan in the nose.

"Oh, sure. I remember now. We had a white elephant table at the school bazaar last year, everything for sale, old, new, some valuable, some junk. Sort of a mini antique shop."

"Correct. Susan Prescott promoted to the first grade. I've got to go, I'm already late for my piano lesson. See you later at the Flea Market maybe."

Joyce skipped down the street tossing the pillow in the

air and catching it. In the middle of the block she turned around and shouted, "Don't miss the orange cupcakes. They are *divine*."

Susan walked slowly up the street thinking, and not about cupcakes either. Maybe she'd go to the Flea Market, maybe she wouldn't. If she did it would be because she wanted to, not because Joyce said to. From now on she'd make up her own mind about things, not listen to anybody.

She stopped in front of the dry cleaner's and looked across the street at St. John's Church. There was a sign on the terrace—*Flea Market Today From Ten Until Five.* People were going up the steps as though it were Easter Sunday instead of a plain ordinary Saturday in October.

It might be fun to go. Who could tell? She might find a bargain, something very nice for fifty cents. Oh, being independent was great. She'd go.

2

The Flea Market

As NOTHING was coming either way, Susan ran across the street, up the steep terrace steps and into St. John's Parish House.

Joyce was right. The Flea Market was great, white elephant tables all over the big room. She elbowed her way through the crowd of grownups and children, "Excuse me, excuse me," and came out in front of a long table made of boards across sawhorses. She could see the sawhorse feet below the purple crepe-paper table cloth.

What a marvelous bunch of things to choose from; handmade aprons, pan holders, teaspoons, forks with yellow handles, cups without saucers, saucers without cups, plates with flowers around the edge, plain plates, some with not a single nick. Mother would like everything, especially that darling music box with the ballet dancer on top.

19

Joyce was wrong about one thing. There *was* a real white elephant, standing between the tea towels and the baby bibs. Catching sight of him, Susan giggled. She had to, he was so cute. Wait until she told Joyce about him, she'd giggle too, a real white elephant on a white elephant table.

He was a stuffed toy elephant about five inches high. His coat was dirty and worn so thin you could see stuffing in two places. One red-lined ear was nearly off, his tail hung by a thread, and his trunk was askew. There was nothing worn-out about his eyes, though; they were shiny black, sharp and bright.

Susan looked at him intently for a long time, then slowly reached out and touched him. Right away, by magic, she knew his story. Brand new he'd been given to a beautiful girl named Debbie by her father who was the best poet there was. One night when Debbie was asleep with the white elephant in her arms a burglar sneaked in, stole him, and gave him to his horrid son. No, Susan shook her head, gave him to his daughter, a horrid girl, horrider than Joyce Gibbs at her worst. That girl played roughly with the toy for years and then, when he was old and worn-out, she got rid of him —just pitched him out and here he was.

How could anybody be so mean? Susan wouldn't give away a single one of her family of stuffed toys. Now and always during the day they were lined up against her pillow: Dolly, the long-legged doll with yellow braids; Rab, a rabbit; Sam Snake, green as Joyce's pillow; Octavia, a pink octopus; and two bears, Ted and Teddy. The bears used to belong to Susan's brother Mike. He was fifteen now, too old for bears, he said. Mike claimed Susan was too old for stuffed toys too, but she wasn't.

Mike teased the daylights out of Susan about her toy family. Teasing her was his favorite indoor sport. His favorite outdoor sport was football and Hugo Scott, captain of the Mt. Washington team, was his hero. Mike was forever talking about Hugo's muscles, saying how great he was. Susan had nothing against muscles. They just weren't everything, that's all.

"Are you interested in buying the elephant?" asked the stylish woman behind the table. "It is twenty-five cents."

"No, thank you," Susan told her. "I'd like to buy him very much but I'm shopping for a birthday present for my mother and I don't think an elephant would do."

"How about the music box?" The woman wound the key on the side of the box and the dancer, dressed in pink tulle, twirled on tiptoe to "Ta, ta, ta, tata," a familiar tune that sounded as though it were being played by a mouse orchestra.

"Yes, that would be perfect," Susan said. "How much does it cost?"

"Two dollars," was the discouraging answer.

"Do you have anything pretty for fifty cents?" Susan asked, wishing the elephant would stop looking at her.

"Tea towels are fifty and the blue linen handkerchief is only twenty-five cents. It's new, worth at least a dollar."

"It is nice, only I hoped to find something fancier. Before I decide I think I'll look at things on some of the other tables. Thank you for helping me."

Susan exchanged glances with the elephant one last time, then turned her back on him and moved on to the next table. It was full of games and records. One game to play with marbles might be fun, though it was more her own type of game than Mother's. What about a book? Mother read all the time.

Susan walked over to the book table and spent at least twenty minutes looking them over. Paperbacks, new and dog-eared, old hardbacks from somebody's bookcase, new books from last Christmas. Whichever one she chose for sure would be one Mother had already read. At last she gave up and crossed the room to the cake table.

How beautiful all the cakes were to see, to smell, and she bet anything to taste. Not to buy, though. Mrs. Benson who lived next door and was one of Mother's best friends was going to bake the birthday cake.

That three-layer chocolate cake looked delicious and so did the white cake next to it and those brownies with lots of nuts in them. On the other side of the brownies was a plateful of orange cupcakes, the ones Joyce Gibbs had said were divine.

Susan rocked back and forth on her heels swinging her pocketbook.

"May I help you?" asked the saleswoman, the organist's sister or the postman's wife, Susan wasn't sure which.

"Just looking, thank you. No, wait. How much are the cupcakes?"

"A dollar a dozen or ten cents apiece."

"They do look good..."

"Mrs. Smith, the minister's wife, made them this morning and she is one of the best cooks in the parish."

"I see. Well, I'll take one."

Susan opened the red pocketbook and counted out ten pennies which she exchanged for the cupcake. She held it in her hand thinking what fun it was to have money of your own to spend and nobody to tell you how to spend it. Then she took a bite, a small one, hoping to make the cupcake last a long time. Another bite, bigger. Joyce was right, it was divine. With the third bite, the cupcake was gone.

She licked her fingers and ran the tip of her tongue around her lips to make sure she hadn't missed any icing, then said politely, "Another one, please."

After all, forty cents was almost as much as fifty and thirty wasn't much less, really.

The second was better than the first, bigger with thicker icing. De-lectable. After watching the clerk sell a dozen brownies to a man holding a small boy in his arms, Susan said, "I'll take one more."

She had to say it, simply had to. Now there were twenty pennies left. Still, twenty cents was almost enough for the blue linen handkerchief which was pretty and would do.

The third and positively last orange cupcake didn't go down as fast as the other two because Susan was so thirsty she had a hard time swallowing. Oh, good, there was a pop stand over in the corner.

"Lemonade, please," she said to a boy about Mike's age wearing a white cap on the side of his head, a butcher's apron tight around slim hips.

"Large or small?"

"Large." Thirsty as Susan was, small wouldn't have done a bit of good. In fact, one large cup wasn't enough; she had to have a second.

"Twenty cents," the boy said when she had finished.

"*Twenty.* You've got to be kidding. *That* much for lemonade?"

"You said large and you bought two cups."

Susan frowned and paid him reluctantly. Every last cent gone and nothing to show for it except a too-sweet feeling inside. She couldn't bear the thought of going home with no present at all for Mother. If only she hadn't eaten that third cupcake—and one glass of lemonade should have been enough.

Susan wandered around in a circle, bumping into people, not saying excuse me or anything. Life was grim and hopeless and couldn't be worse. Yes it could. Here came Joyce Gibbs, still carrying that monstrous pillow.

3

The White Elephant

"THERE YOU ARE, Susan," Joyce said, bounding over. "I knew you'd come to the Flea Market after I told you about it. Isn't it great? I was so late for my music lesson I missed it altogether, and is my mother going to be furious when she finds out. What did you buy for your mother?"

"Nothing yet. There are so many things to choose from it isn't easy to decide."

Susan would rather die than have Joyce find out she'd eaten the birthday money. Looking at her feet, she said, "There is a pretty blue linen handkerchief I know Mother would like."

"A handkerchief? Is that all?"

"It's a bargain, reduced, worth much more. Come on with me and I'll show it to you. I'll show you something else too, Joyce, a real white elephant. You said there weren't any, but you were wrong."

27

"You're kidding."

"I am not. Come on, you'll see."

Susan led the way to the sawhorse table thinking to herself that if Joyce were a different kind of person, somebody you could trust, she'd ask to borrow twenty-five cents from her. Joyce being Joyce, though, she'd want to know why, and if she ever found out Susan would never hear the end of it and by tomorrow the whole town would know. She decided she wouldn't borrow one cent from that girl even if she were starving.

Where was the white elephant? Susan didn't see him. Hands on her hips she looked quickly up and down the table. He wasn't there. She looked again slowly, not skipping over things, up, down, across, back. No sign of him.

"What became of the little white elephant?" she asked the saleswoman who was busy trying to put a large something or other into a too-small secondhand paper bag for another customer. "He was right here a while ago." She smacked her hand down on the table to show the exact spot.

"I expect it's gotten under something," the woman answered without looking up. "No wonder you can't find the toy the way people have been handling things."

"Then he hasn't been sold?"

"I don't think so. A boy wanted to buy it for his baby brother, then decided it was too soiled. I'll help you hunt for it as soon as I have the time."

Susan didn't wait. She lifted a yellow apron hopefully. The elephant was not underneath. She picked up a lamp shade. Not there either. He wasn't under the lace tablecloth or behind the brass vase or anywhere.

"Why all the to-do over some dirty old toy?" asked Joyce, not helping at all. "You certainly don't want to buy it for your mother."

"Of course not," Susan answered, clipping her words off short and keeping on with the search like a hound with his nose on a scent. "I just want to find him, that's all."

"Why?"

"Because I do, Joyce. People don't have to have a reason for everything."

"I suppose not, only a girl your age getting worked up over a toy seems sort of silly to me. Say," she pointed to a gray-white tail sticking out from under the edge of the purple tablecloth, "is that what you're looking for?"

"Yes."

Susan pounced on the tail and whisked out the little white elephant chanting, "I found him, I found him, he was lost and I found him."

"I'm the one who found it," declared Joyce, admiring her pillow, smiling at it as she spoke, "and I wouldn't touch the dirty old thing if you paid me. Put it down, Susan, you'll get germs. It belongs in the garbage can if you ask me."

"Nobody did ask you and he does *not* belong in the gar-

bage can," snapped Susan. Joyce made her so mad some-
times and this was one of those times. She was glad when
Joyce saw a friend over by the door and hailed her, "Hey,
Mary Ellen!"

Joyce darted off, tossing "See you around, Susan," over
her shoulder.

Not if Susan could help it she wouldn't. She'd seen
enough of Joyce for one day. Imagine saying the dear little
white elephant belonged in a garbage can. Mean, that's what
Joyce was, just plain mean.

She wished she hadn't eaten the third cupcake and the
second lemonade and not only because of the money spent,
either. Her insides felt melancholy, so did her brains. Seeing
a small antique rocking chair in the middle of the room, a
SOLD sign hanging on its back, she sat down in it, feet
close together, her own back straight.

All of her planning, earning money, being on her own,
had come to nothing. Mother's birthday tomorrow and nothing to give her. That was terrible. She knew what kind of a
girl she was—selfish, greedy, and what about the white
elephant? She hated to go off and leave him to some dire
fate such as a garbage can.

A magician could save him and she was one. To test her
secret powers she laid the empty pocketbook on her lap and
grabbed the chair seat under her with both hands. At once
the rocking chair told her its sad story.

Years ago it belonged to a beautiful lady with long gold-en hair — no, black ringlets. Anyway, she was married to a prince in disguise. They had a beautiful baby boy, then the prince died. It was very sad. The baby grew up. First, though, he was rocked to sleep every night in the rocking chair. When he was a man he became president of a bank and had lots of money for fine and fancy furniture and the rocker languished in the attic until —

"Hello, Susan," a low throaty voice said, bringing the chair's story to an abrupt end.

Susan jumped to her feet and backed away, covering her mouth with her hands, the red pocketbook falling on the floor.

There, standing right in front of her, was Mrs. Gaffney.

4

The Gaffney Debt

"WHAT IS the matter, child?" Mrs. Gaffney asked. "You look as if you'd seen a ghost."

Susan was too scared to answer. A witch was worse than a ghost, and Mrs. Gaffney really must be a witch. Susan was sure now. One second the old woman hadn't been there. Then suddenly—*pouff*—she appeared out of nowhere.

Mrs. Gaffney leaned over to set her heavy shopping bag on the floor, saying, "Something is obviously bothering you. Since you won't say what it is, I'll take a guess. Money. Am I right?"

Susan frowned and took another step back. Mrs. Gaffney wasn't guessing. She knew the way witches knew about things. She knew.

Opening her large black pocketbook, Mrs. Gaffney said, "Let me help. How much do you need?"

Susan shook her head no, but a vision of the white elephant appeared inside her head and it wouldn't take no for an answer. She swallowed twice and said in a small voice, "I need twenty-five cents." She wanted to ask for more but held back because Mother didn't approve of borrowing unless absolutely necessary. Although a present for your mother was necessary, it wasn't *absolutely* necessary. The elephant was.

After fumbling around in the pocketbook with her bony old hand, Mrs. Gaffney found a quarter and held it out to Susan, saying, "There you are."

Susan took the money quickly, gingerly, almost snatching it rudely. "Thank you very much," she said. "I'll pay you back a week from today at the latest."

Mrs. Gaffney nodded and Susan started to leave, took three steps, turned, and said, "I appreciate the loan very much and if you keep it a secret I'll appreciate it double much."

Mrs. Gaffney nodded again, picking up her shopping bag. Susan, money in her hot, damp hand headed for the sawhorse table at full speed. "Oh, excuse me, Mrs. Smith. I was going so fast I didn't see you at all."

Now where was the elephant? She whisked a lamp shade into the air and there he was, just where she'd left him. She picked him up, gave him a fierce hug and bought him, paying for him with the Gaffney quarter.

"May I have something to put him in, please? Thank you." Susan dropped the elephant into a secondhand paper bag. He was hers forever, rescued from nobody knew what, safe and loved from now on. He must have a name at once.

Over by the window in the corner away from other people she opened the bag and looked at him lying in the bottom, feet and trunk in the air. Now let's see—David, John, James, Paul, were all good male names and for sure he was a boy elephant. Anybody could tell he wasn't a girl; there was something about the look in his eyes. "Trunko," Susan said aloud. Yes, Trunko was the right name for him.

Pleased as could be, Susan raised her head and there looking at her with definite disapproval was plump Mrs. Benson, next door neighbor and sitter for Susan when Mother was out, which she often was. Mother was a freelance writer and when she was doing research on something at the library downtown or over in Washington, Susan stayed with Mrs. Benson.

"So there you are, Susan Prescott," Mrs. Benson said in a tone with an edge to it. "Your poor mother has been worried half to death looking for you all over Mt. Washington for the past hour and a half, and here you are enjoying yourself at the fair. Some people are so thoughtless."

"I was naming my elephant," Susan declared, trying to defend herself. "Besides, Mother told me to take my time. I'm leaving now."

She started to run to the door, Mrs. Benson calling after her, "The last time I saw your poor mother she was talking to a policeman in front of the A&P."

Susan wished Mrs. Benson hadn't said your poor mother. She hated it when people said things like that, and Mrs. Benson had said it twice.

Susan left the Parish House fast, flew down the terrace steps, looked both ways to make sure nothing was coming, dashed across the street, and ran on down the hill.

There was Mother getting into the seven-year-old Volkswagen, parked across from the grocery store. Maybe Mrs. Benson was right to say what she had. Even Mother's back looked worried.

"Mo-ther!" Susan shouted. "Wait for me!"

Mrs. Prescott swung around, her face looking both worried and furious, mostly furious. "Susan, where *have* you been?" she demanded to know.

"Shopping," Susan said, racing across the street, empty pocketbook swinging, full brown paper bag clutched tightly in her other hand. "You knew I was going shopping, and you said to take my time."

"I didn't mean take all day. It's after two o'clock."

"It couldn't be *that* late."

"Well, it is. Get in the car at once."

Mother didn't often speak sharply but when she did, Susan hopped. On the way home she said, "Drive faster,

Mother. The football game starts at two, I mean started at two. We'll miss the whole first quarter if we don't hurry."

"We're not going."

"Not going at all? Why not? Mike may play in the last quarter. He said Hugo didn't actually promise to put him in but he hinted that he might and Hugo isn't a hinter so it's nearly a sure thing."

"We are not going," Mother repeated. "I've had all I can take for one day, police looking for you, everybody looking for you and feeling sorry for me. I've had more than enough."

Susan was silent for a while then, hoping to clear the air, she rattled on and on about meeting Joyce Gibbs, going to the Flea Market, and seeing a million things for sale. She did not mention cupcakes, the Gaffney debt, or Trunko. Later on when she was sure the air was clear she'd introduce him.

The car stopped by the white front gate. Susan jumped out, ran up the path, into the house, and down the hall to the kitchen where she put the brown paper bag on top of the refrigerator for the time being. As she did so, a wave of something extremely uncomfortable engulfed her, part sorrow, part shame, a wicked feeling. No present for Mother on her birthday, not even a card.

Would the joy of owning the white elephant balance things? Susan didn't know. Nothing was clearly this or that anymore. For a second she wished she were six years old again. Only for a second.

Mother was coming in now. Susan hated to be on the outs with her for two reasons. First, of course, she was Mother and then, as a person, she was strong, responsible, smart, and pretty too, in a tailored, straightforward, chin-up way. How could Dad leave her and go off with somebody else he hardly knew?

"You must be hungry," Mother said, the pinched look beginning to fade from her face. "I am. I was too worried to eat when I fixed lunch for Mike. I'll make us a sandwich."

"Nothing for me, thank you," Susan said. "I'm not the least bit hungry." That did it. She burst into tears. She was not a weeper but her stomach felt terrible and so did the rest of her, especially her mind and her conscience.

With Mother's arm around her—and Mother was not usually the touching type—Susan confessed. Not everything, of course, just the part about earning the money for the birthday present. Leaving out the cupcakes and the loan from Mrs. Gaffney, she ended the confession with a burst of emotion, saying, "And with the money I bought *this!*"

Snatching the paper bag off of the refrigerator, she opened it, pulled out the little white elephant, and said, "His name is Trunko Prescott. I *had* to buy him."

Mother took Trunko from Susan with two fingers and held him out at arms length. As she turned him slowly, looking at him from all sides, a smile spread over her face.

"Of course you had to buy him, Susan," she said. "He's charming, a perfect birthday present. I'd rather have him than anything I can think of."

"You would?" Susan said weakly, feeling absolutely horrible.

5

The Birthday Present

SUSAN HADN'T DREAMED her mother would want Trunko for a present. This was a new twist to things and she didn't like it one bit. She wanted Trunko for herself, more than anything. She couldn't say so, though. Nobody could be *that* selfish.

Although Susan didn't give the faintest hint of the way she felt, Mother got the message, and she was not the magician type either. Mother was the rock solid, feet on the ground, dependable type. She had to be, with Dad gone, but she was even before he left, and he admired her for it—said so when he was home on a visit.

Dad wasn't dependable. You never knew what he was going to do or when he was going to do it. Once he came to see them without saying he was coming and nobody was home. All that distance just to leave a note under the door knocker. Susan knew that note by heart—*Sorry to miss everybody see you two weeks from today. Love Dad.* But he didn't come. Mother and Susan had fixed a special dinner, everything he liked, hot biscuits and all, and he never showed up. A letter arrived the next day saying he was sorry he couldn't make it.

Once Mother overheard Susan and Mike talking about Dad, saying how mean he was to leave and how unreliable he was, and did she put her foot down hard. Susan would never forget it. Mother said they didn't know the first thing about how difficult it was to live, and until they did they were to speak respectfully of their father, was that clear?

It was.

Now Mother said, "The elephant can be ours, Susan, yours and mine."

"Fine," was Susan's quick answer. "He needs a bath."

Mother agreed. She sloshed Trunko up and down quickly in thick suds while Susan watched.

Before the elephant had time to get soggy, Mother pulled him out of the water. Susan patted him dry with a Turkish towel, then laid him on a dry towel on the living room windowsill. He looked so funny, fur or whatever it was plastered down, the red lining of his ears showing through pink on the backs. Now and then during the afternoon Susan turned him over to let the sun shine on his other side.

At ten minutes of six Mike came home. One look at his

face and Susan didn't need to ask how the game turned out but she asked anyway.

"Thirty-four to nothing in their favor," Mike answered dolefully. "A bust, and all Hugo's fault. He was awful, didn't do one thing right."

"Did you play, Mike?"

"Nope. I woulda, only Hugo put Pete Griffith in instead. I shoulda played in Hugo's place. Talk about a flop. I never thought I'd see the day when he would—"

Mike stopped midsentence, pointed a finger at the elephant, and yelled, "Call the exterminators!"

"He's Mother's birthday present from me," Susan explained. "His name is Trunko."

"Wow, some present," sputtered Mike. "What's Mom gonna do with it—plug a drain?"

"She likes him for himself and so do I. He's had a bath. As soon as he gets dry you'll like him too. He'll be perfectly dry in time for the birthday party."

He was. Suppertime the next day, when Mrs. Benson came in with the birthday cake, forty candles on it, Trunko was standing on the sideboard, coat brushed, tail sewed back on, ear tight, patches over the holes so the stuffing couldn't come out, red ribbon from last Christmas tied around his neck.

Mike almost spoiled things by saying that even if the

elephant were studded with diamonds it was a stupid present to give a grown woman, which Susan said was a real Joyce Gibbs remark.

Mother said something about some people liking football, others liking elephants, then everybody sang to her and she cut the cake. Susan enjoyed the singing and would have enjoyed the cake if it hadn't come so soon after the cupcakes. It was a beautiful cake and deserved more than nibbling. Mike wanted to know if she was sick or something, eating like a bird, and Mother got up and felt her forehead to see if she had a fever.

Susan had been to cheerier birthday parties. She remembered one in particular, hers, a costume party three years ago. Dad had worn a false mustache that drooped and a goofy hat with pompons on top. Two months later he was gone.

Anyway, she had Trunko. Mother had him too, which was very good. She said she liked him best of her presents and she got a bunch: new white gloves from her sister in North Carolina, writing paper from Mike, a blue blouse from an aunt in Florida, the cake from Mrs. Benson, and a lot of cards. One postmarked St. Louis, Mo. felt more like a letter to Susan. From Dad, she bet, though she couldn't be sure because the address was typewritten.

Bedtime was great. Mother let Susan take Trunko up to

sleep with her. Lying in the double bed, lights out, her family of stuffed toys around her, Susan felt blissful.

Not for long. She sat up. Was that Mrs. Gaffney sitting on the chair in the corner? No, silly, it was just a lumpy dark shadow. She wished she didn't owe Mrs. Gaffney twenty-five cents, mainly because to pay off the debt she'd have to go to her shop, and she didn't want to go there ever. She'd pay soon and then never go near the old woman again. Still, if it weren't for Mrs. Gaffney she wouldn't own Trunko.

She hugged him, snuggled under the covers, and was just drifting off to sleep when the telephone rang. Curious, she sat up in bed to listen. She heard Mother say "Yes, she did, Mrs. Smith. I see. What a shame. Yes, I understand—a mistake like that could happen to anyone. I am sorry too, very sorry. She is so enthusiastic about it. We'll straighten things out in the morning. Good night."

Susan hopped out of bed, spilling Rab, Ted, and Dolly on the floor, ran to the head of the stairs, and called down, "What was that all about, Mother?"

"Mrs. Smith, the wife of the Rector at St. John's, says there has been a mixup over one of the donations to the Flea Market. Go to sleep. I'll tell you the details in the morning."

"No. Tell me now, please."

"The elephant was not supposed to be sold. A mother,

Mrs. Smith did not give her name, thought her son had out-grown the toy and donated it along with a boxful of other things. Evidently the mother was wrong, for the boy is up-set and grieving, so Mrs. Smith says. Someone is coming in the morning to discuss the situation with you."

"There is nothing to discuss," Susan declared in a loud, firm voice. "Not one thing. I bought Trunko and he is mine. I mean ours. I'm keeping him no matter what, and that is final."

She ran back to her room, scooped up the toys that had fallen to the floor, tossed them on the mussed bed, jumped in herself, and pulled the covers over her head.

While she was still underneath the tent, Mike came home from wherever it was he'd been. He was always going some-where to study with somebody or play records or talk foot-ball. She heard him say goodnight to Mother and come clomping upstairs, making as much noise as ten ponies.

He walked down the hall to her door, poked his head in, and bawled, "Waaaaaaaaaaaaaaaa!" Then, holding his nose to give his voice an Englishman-with-a-cold voice, he said, "Hark, do I hear the trumpeting of an elephant?"

Mother must have told him to stop teasing because right away he said, "Okay. I'll let her alone if you insist." Then, through the door again, "Good night, Sweetie Pie and Whatshisname."

A muffled good night came from the mound of covers.

It was not a good night for Susan. She tossed and turned, gritted her teeth, and worried. So some stupid child was grieving for her elephant. So what? That was *his* hard luck. Let people come in the morning. She was ready for them.

6

Stanley Trunko

WHEN MORNING CAME, the bears, the rabbit, the doll, the octopus, the snake, the white elephant, and most of the covers were on the floor.

During breakfast Susan and Mother couldn't get a word in, Mike was so wound up over football. "Hugo had a bad day Saturday, that's all," chew, chew, chew. "Everybody does once in a while. Bound to. You can't win em all." Another large forkful of scrambled eggs and he went on. "If St. Paul's beats Severn and we beat Forest Park we'll still be in the running for first place because Forest Park beat Severn last Saturday, the day Friends beat us on account of Hugo. Get it?"

"No, I *don't,*" said Susan, buttering a slice of toast. She hated things like that, things you couldn't figure out for the life of you. "There's the doorbell. You go, Mike. I'll bet anything it's those people about Trunko."

47

Mike dropped his fork on the floor, knocked over his chair, picked it up, and finally made it to the door.

Susan stopped chewing toast to listen, Mother did too, and they were surprised to hear Mike say, "Hi ya, Hugo. Come in, come in. What brings you to our humble abode at pink of dawn?" And they nearly flipped, at least Susan nearly did, when Hugo's voice boomed, "I came to see your sister."

"My *sister!*" Mike exclaimed, as though anyone who wanted to see Susan must be crazy. "What the heck do you want to see her for?"

Hugo's answer to that was more surprising still. "My business with her is private, Prescott, if you don't mind."

"I see," Mike said, though he didn't. All he knew was that he was not wanted. He returned to the dining room and flopped in his chair, saying coolly to Susan, "Hugo Scott wants to see you about something."

Susan practically fell into the hall, with Mother two steps behind. There stood Hugo, the mighty Hugo. Even without shoulder pads his dimensions were spectacular.

"Good morning, Susan," he said, holding out the hand that held the fate of the Mt. Washington football team in its palm.

"Good morning, Hugo," Susan said, shaking the hand. Ouch, what a grip. "My brother says you want to see me."

"Correct." Hugo ran his fingers through his hair twice

and called out in a loud boom, "Come on back, Prescott. You might as well hear what I have to say from the beginning. You're sure to hear it anyhow."

After much chair scraping and banging around, Mike arrived at the hall door just as Hugo said, looking straight at Susan, "I've come for Stanley."

"Stanley?"

"Yep, old Stanley, my elephant."

Mike's eyebrows shot upward and his jaw dropped, and Susan said, "*You* are the child who is grieving?"

"Obviously I am not a child," declared Hugo, swelling out his chest. He rubbed his hands together searching for the right words to say. "Grieving? Well, let's say—well, yes, grieving and angry."

He paced up and down the hall. "My mother had no right to give Stanley away to be sold, no right to even touch him." Whereupon Mrs. Prescott said, "There must have been a misunderstanding, Hugo. I'm sure your mother would not go against your wishes deliberately."

Hugo, paying no attention to that remark, faced Susan squarely and said, "You do have him, don't you? Mrs. Smith told my mother that your mother said you did."

Susan took her time answering. She paced a bit herself, hands behind her back, before she said in an offhand manner, "I bought an elephant at St. John's Flea Market and presented him to my mother on her birthday—half of him, that is. The other half is mine. Whether he happens to be your elephant, I wouldn't know. After all, there must be thousands of white elephants in the world, maybe more. Mine's name is Trunko."

Mother mentioned that it was getting late, time for school, but her words were drowned out by Hugo's, "Get him, Susan, please. I've got to know whether the elephant you bought is Stanley or not."

Mike opened his mouth to say something but swallowed instead as Susan started slowly up the steps. She walked slowly down the upstairs hall to her room and dug Trunko out of the nest of covers beside the bed. Holding him tenderly with both hands, trunk front, she walked slowly downstairs again.

"Stanley!" exclaimed Hugo before she reached the bottom step. "He's been spruced up, but it's Stanley all right. I'd know him anywhere."

Susan felt very confused. She said to Mother, "Do we have to give him up?" and Mother answered, "I'll let you decide, dear," such a maddening thing to say.

After a long pause during which Mike cleared his throat over and over again—enough to remove his tonsils, Susan thought—she looked up at Hugo and asked, "Does Stanley sleep with you?"

At that Mike's face got so red Susan was afraid he was going to burst, but before he had a chance to Hugo said, "Not now." Mike looked somewhat relieved and more so when Hugo explained, "Now that I am no longer a child Stanley stays on top of my desk, or did until day before yesterday."

In a magic flash Susan saw clearly the life and love of Hugo Scott and Stanley. It was a touching drama, full of pathos. At least she thought it was full of pathos, though the meaning of the word was not clear in her mind. Anyway, it was a beautiful story and how it ended was up to her.

She hugged Trunko with both arms, feeling the heavy weight of making a decision all by herself. She rocked him this way and that, her eyes stinging. She must give him up no matter how much it hurt.

Thrusting Trunko straight out she said, "Here, take him and put him back where he belongs." She was glad Mother had gone into the kitchen where she could hear what was said and at the same time not be in on the painful giving up.

It was painful. Trunko was so cute and Susan loved him so.

Hugo stuffed him head down in the pocket of his jacket. Then he opened his wallet, took out a five-dollar bill and offered it to Susan, saying, "A small reward for Stanley who is worth a million dollars to me."

"No, thank you," she said with dignity, chin in the air, "I would not give him up for money." The thought crossed her mind to accept twenty-five cents, the borrowed purchase price. However, she dismissed it at once; not to take a cent was worthier.

From Mike's expression he obviously thought anybody who turned down five bucks was nutty. Hugo understood, though. He smiled at Susan and said, "Good girl," then turned to Mike. "Sorry I let the team down Saturday. With Stanley gone I couldn't keep my mind on the game. Now that he's back, thanks to your sister, we'll clobber them this Saturday."

After a "Yeah team" from Mike, Hugo said, "Get your gear together, Prescott, I'll drive you to school. My mother lent me the family car today as a peace offering. Care to ride with us, Susan?"

"No, thank you, Hugo. Mother will take me. If you want to do something I'd like, though, call Stanley Trunko sometimes."

"Right you are. From now on he's Stanley Trunko," Hugo said, nearly shaking Susan's hand off. Turning, he raised his voice to Mike, who was upstairs in his room by now. "Snap it up, Prescott, we haven't got all day."

As Mike bounded down the steps, Hugo added, "I want to drop old S.T. off at my house on the way. *You* understand how I feel about him but some of the other guys might not."

Mike, flattered to be singled out by his hero, followed him out the door. As the two of them crossed the porch Susan heard Hugo say, "I just thought of something to give your sister. I'll surprise her with it as soon as I can catch it."

Catch what? Susan wondered. Standing still in the hall, she speculated about it. A turtle? No, anybody could catch a turtle right off. Maybe it was a snake, a harmless snake with a yellow collar around its neck.

"Hurry, Susan," Mother said, shaking the car keys nervously.

Susan flew upstairs, cleaned her teeth, brushed her hair, and flew down again. This once she left her room in chaos and empty without Trunko. He really had made a place for himself in a short time. She was going to miss him.

Mother was going to miss him too. She said so as they got into the car. She also said she was proud of Susan for giving him up.

Riding along on the way to school there was a warm, friendly silence between them. Susan had things on her mind, though. With Trunko gone, Mother had no birthday present from her after all—not even half of one. The Gaffney debt still had to be paid too.

Susan hoped Hugo would hurry and catch whatever it was he planned to give her. She wanted it now, right away —not that it or anything else would take Trunko's place.

What was it Hugo had in mind? She could try magic to find out. Better not, that might scare away whatever it was. Better just wait impatiently.

7

Sereena

THAT DAY was a plain usual Monday for Susan: math, spelling, recess, reading, lunch, library, social studies, art, and a short lecture by Miss Buffington at closing time about how one boy had no right to disrupt the whole class.

After school she didn't do anything in particular, just played outdoors with the other children in the neighborhood: Amy who lived in the white house on top of the hill, the Digman boys next door to her, and a new girl from the other side of Bensons'.

During the evening Susan made plans to pay off the Gaffney debt. Tuesday after supper she'd get her regular allowance for the week, seventy-five cents. Twenty-five was for milk at lunch, five cents a day. Ten cents went for Sunday School, and ten more into the pink pig for college. The rest was for ice cream cones, chocolate bars, contributions to worthy causes, and other living expenses.

This week she'd pay the debt and starve between meals. She'd go to Gaffney's antique shop on Wednesday, rap on the door, hand over the twenty-five cents she owed, and scram fast. Nothing dire could happen to her in that short a time, could it?

Because it was raining, Susan went straight home after school on Tuesday. Football practice was canceled, so Mike came home early too. Susan could hear him in his room putting up a shelf or something. She could also hear Mother typing, tap, tap, tap, in the upstairs study and rain tapping on the roof. Then at four o'clock by the kitchen clock, while Susan was fixing herself a peanut butter and jelly snack, she heard a car stop out front and footsteps coming up the path.

Could it be Hugo? She ran into the hall and opened the front door. There he stood in a wet yellow slicker, a grin on his face and in his arms a thin, gray cat with a long, thin, gray tail.

One look at that cat and Susan's insides expanded like a balloon to make room for a boundless love.

"A present for you, Susan, from Stanley and me," Hugo said, holding the cat out to her. "Somebody must have dumped her out of a car or something. She's been hanging around our block for two weeks and more. The S.P.C.A. came twice to pick her up but she wouldn't let the men catch her. I only could because she went under our porch to get out of the rain—you know how cats hate rain. I cornered her, and here she is, all yours if you want her and your mother says it's okay to keep her."

"I want her," Susan said, taking the cat gingerly in her arms because of claws. "What's her name, Hugo?"

"Who knows? You name her."

"Sereena," Susan said at once. The name suited the cat perfectly.

She hugged Sereena, saying, "From this moment on until the end of time I'll defend her against all odds." She took a deep breath, having used up all she had, and added, "Thank you, Hugo, and thank Stanley Trunko for me. I'll take her up to my room now. Mike is upstairs, go on up."

"Another time. My mother is in the car, came along to hold the cat, and she wants to get back home right away. I'm glad you like the cat. I was pretty sure you would after the way you took to Stanley."

"Stanley Trunko."

"Stanley Trunko it is," Hugo said. "Got to push off. See you."

The front door slammed and footsteps went down the path again, but oh how different the world was since they had come to the door.

"Who was that, dear?" Mother called from upstairs.

"Hugo Scott," Susan answered, a wild, fierce feeling sweeping over her. "He brought me a present. Her name is Sereena."

Mike thundered down the steps, landing in the hall with such a crash-bang that Sereena leaped out of Susan's arms, fled into the living room, and dived under the couch.

"Now look what you did," Susan scolded. "You scared the daylights out of my cat."

"Your what?" exclaimed Mother on her way downstairs.

"My cat Sereena, a present from Hugo and Trunko. She's a girl and from the looks of her she has had a hard life and needs rest, plenty of cat food, and lots of love."

"I do not want to hear one word more about any cat," Mother said firmly, eyes flashing fire. "There will be *no* cat in this house now or at any other time, and that is final."

"I'm sorry you feel that way, Mother," Susan said calmly, dropping down on her knees and poking her head under the couch. "It is too late to change things. Sereena is already mine. Here kitty, kitty. Come on, darling. Susan won't hurt you. Come on."

"Pretty decent of Hugo to go to the trouble of catching it and bringing it here," Mike said.

Mother lit into him and Susan. "You both know perfectly well that cats are not allowed on this hill because it is part of the bird sanctuary. Besides, I don't like cats."

"I like them," said Susan, pulling Sereena out from under the couch by a hind leg.

"There will be *no* cat in this house," Mother said. "Anything else, but not a cat. You'll have to get rid of that one at once."

Susan stood up, the cat in her arms, and glared at her mother with anger.

"Big deal," Mike said gloomily. "Close as I am to playing first string and my sister is forced to dispose of Hugo's generous gift. Real big deal."

Mother, a little calmer now, changed her tone. "We'll find another home for the cat. Any place except here."

Susan also changed her tone and said sweetly, "Almost more than anything I want to please you, Mother. This once I can't. I have dedicated the rest of my life to Sereena. You wouldn't want your daughter to be the kind of person who didn't do what she'd dedicated her life to do, would you?"

"When you live in your own home and pay your own bills, you may make the decisions. Until then, I have a say. Is that clear?"

Susan nodded, tears stinging her eyes, and Mother went on, "The cat can stay here for a few days while we try to find a good home for her. But if we don't find one by the end of the week, I'll call the S.P.C.A."

Tears ran down Susan's cheeks. Mike ran his fingers through his long hair. Mother went out into the kitchen and began banging pans around.

Susan said to Mike, "She and I were so close, owning the elephant together, losing him together. And now—"

"I get your point," Mike told her, starting up the steps. Half way he stopped, turned around, and reminded Susan that it wasn't easy for Mother to manage the house and family by herself. And before going on to his room he said, "Cheer up, Sis, anything can happen in a week."

He was right. A week was a long time.

Feeling faintly hopeful again because of that, Susan carried Sereena up to her room and laid her gently on the bed. She looked marvelous there surrounded by Dolly, Rab, and the rest, even more marvelous than Trunko.

Susan shook her head no, not wanting to be disloyal to the elephant. It was Sereena's being alive that made the difference. She knelt beside the bed and pushed her hand, palm up, under the warm, soft cat and felt the faint, rapid beating of her heart.

Being alive was pure magic, it really was. Susan wooed her own magic, asking for the cat's story and here it came right into her head. She didn't tell it out loud, just let it flow in silence:

Far away in China, or maybe in France—yes, in France —six kittens were born in the attic of a palace under a slanting roof. While still quite young the most beautiful kitten of them all was snatched from the pink satin-lined basket where she'd been living with three brothers and two sisters by a witch who looked a lot like Mrs. Gaffney. The witch brought her to America by broom or airplane, landing near Baltimore, Maryland. Shortly after landing the kitten escaped from the witch and set out alone to seek her fortune.

By this time Sereena had gone to sleep, so trusting, so dear. A week wasn't much time but it would have to do. Susan, still on her knees beside the bed, went on with the story.

The middle part during which the kitten grew to be a cat was dramatic and perilous, with many nearlys — she was nearly run over by a truck, nearly caught by a big dog, she nearly starved, and nearly froze to death in winter. And from time to time she had innumerable kittens that doubled her joy and quadrupled her problems.

When all seemed lost, the bedraggled, worn-out, homeless cat was rescued by a football player named Hugo who gave her to a girl named Susan Prescott. The end of the story, the and-so-they-lived-happily-ever-after, depended upon Susan and she better get going. When Sereena woke up she'd need food, water, and a sandbox.

Susan got to her feet and left the room, being careful to shut the door securely. A week was not long. She must act swiftly and think clearly. The cat's story positively *must* have a happy ending. She'd die if it didn't.

8

Something Has
to Be Done

TUNA FISH from the pantry, milk from the refrigerator, a sandbox and sand to go in it donated by the youngest Digman boy, and Sereena was all set. She was to sleep with Susan on the foot of the bed, a perfect place for a cat.

What to do next?

After much thinking Susan decided the best thing to do for the time being was nothing, just let nature take its course. As soon as Mother got acquainted with Sereena, saw how well behaved she was, how little trouble, how clean, she'd change her mind and let her stay.

In case an emergency turned up, such as cat food to buy, Susan would postpone paying her debt to Mrs. Gaffney — just until things straightened out and got to be certain.

Wednesday after school Susan tied a blue ribbon around Sereena's neck, tight enough so it wouldn't slip over her head, loose enough to be comfortable. Then she took her outdoors for what was supposed to be a walk, only Sereena kept backing, wouldn't go forward at all. So Susan gave up, took her indoors again and stayed upstairs with her until supper time so she wouldn't get lonesome.

Thursday after school Susan found some doll clothes stuffed in the corner of her underwear drawer and, to entertain Sereena, she dressed her in a full skirt, a plaid cape, and a bonnet tied under her chin. It was not a success. Too much long cat hung down, the clothes were too frivolous for Sereena's personality, the cat's expression was cold, and her tail twitched on the end with disapproval.

Friday Susan let Sereena alone, just sat on the rug beside her, understanding how the cat felt. She and Sereena both wanted a secure home and complete independence at the same time.

How wise Sereena was. Look in her eyes and you could tell she knew more than you did. Susan stroked her tenderly, leaning down over her close enough to see faint stripes, gray on gray, very subtle and artistic. A long, smart, subtle artistic cat, not like any other cat in the world. Who could resist her?

Mother, that's who. Saturday morning Mother's jaw was set in a firm no cat line and there was no sign of relenting in her eyes. After a solemn breakfast with just the two of them —Mike was sleeping late—Susan went up to her room to make plans, her own jaw set. Something had to be done at once. Mother had said Saturday was the deadline and it was Saturday.

Susan stood in the middle of her room and looked around. Everything was pretty, pink bedspread, pink rug, pale pink walls, white ruffled curtains, family of stuffed toys all the colors of the rainbow. If only Trunko were there. Susan felt an ache for him but now was not the time for that. Sereena sunning herself on the desk in front of the window was the target—Sereena and more time.

Mrs. Benson wouldn't keep her for even a day. Amy couldn't because she too lived in the bird park. What about Mary Kent who lived up Falls Road a half a mile? She loved animals and was a friend. No, that German shepherd of Mary's would catch Sereena fast and that would be that.

Hugo would keep her, only she didn't like to ask him because he was the one who'd given her the cat. Who was left? Only Joyce Gibbs. She'd have to take Sereena over to Joyce's house and leave her there for, say, a week. She didn't want to, Joyce being Joyce, but she couldn't think of any place else. She would go right now.

She picked up Sereena, an armful, and carried her downstairs. At the front door she called out, "I'll be home for lunch, Mother. I'm going over to Joyce Gibbs' house on business. Okay?"

"Be careful. I'll take you if you like," Mother answered from upstairs.

"No, thank you. I have Sereena with me, and under the circumstances I'd rather go alone."

"Well, good luck."

Susan went out the door in a huff. Mother's "good luck" meant good luck getting rid of the cat. Mean, rude, heartless, that's what she was. Holding Sereena close, a bit too tight for comfort, Susan walked down the path, down Bird Lane, and on down Falls Road. Thank goodness Mrs. Gaffney didn't see her.

She hurried on her way, crossed the bridge, passed school, walked the three more blocks to Joyce's house and rang the bell. Waiting for somebody to come, she shifted Sereena to her shoulder and held her there the way you hold a baby.

Joyce came to the door and did the rudest thing. She laughed, pointing a finger at Sereena as she said, "Where the heck did you get *that?* Honestly, Susan, you do pick up the craziest things. First a dirty old toy elephant and now that miserable cat."

Susan glared at her, biting her tongue to keep from telling her off. After all, when you are about to ask somebody for a favor you can't do that. She got control of herself, then explained the situation and asked Joyce if she would please keep her cat for a few days.

Well, Joyce was ruder still. "Impossible," she said. "My mother raises purebred Siamese cats. We couldn't think of letting them associate with an alley cat. They might get fleas. Take her to the S.P.C.A. where she belongs."

Susan, simply furious, said, "Sereena does not have fleas. She's as clean as you are, Joyce Gibbs, cleaner, because she grooms herself every single day, sometimes twice a day. And she does *not* belong at the S.P.C.A."

She started to leave, saying in a low, throaty, almost Gaffney voice, "Before I'd let my cat end up at the S.P.C.A. I'd run away with her to the ends of the earth."

Then, shifting Sereena to the other shoulder, she left Joyce's house, her feet pounding the pavement hard, she was so angry.

She did not know what to do. She did not know where to go. Not home, that was sure, not yet. She hadn't given up.

Thinking of home, she thought about her mother and that made her angrier still. Mother just used that off-limits-to-cats stuff as an excuse. She didn't want Sereena to live at their house. She hated cats and Susan hated her for hating them. She really did. Not all the time, just in bolts.

She walked two blocks fast, her temper cooling slightly. Before long she and Sereena were passing St. John's Church, so full of memories of Trunko. Susan stopped and stood thinking. Why not go in and ask for help? Wasn't the church the place where people were supposed to go when they were in trouble? It was, and she was in trouble, deep trouble.

She went in and came right out again. Mr. Smith was in conference, the secretary said; he'd be glad to see her on Monday at three. Susan needed help now.

Not knowing what else to do, she decided to go home for a rest. Her arms ached and Sereena was getting restless. Yes, a rest, then she'd start out again. At Falls Road and the bridge she had to stop for a red light and there stopped also, headed the other way, was Mother in the Volks.

"Get in the car this minute, Susan," Mother ordered, head out the window. "The very idea, running away from home."

"Running away!"

"Yes. Joyce telephoned a while ago to tell me you were going to run away with the cat."

"You wait'll I get her," Susan said, never madder. " I did *not* say I was going to run away. I merely said I would before I'd let Sereena go to the S.P.C.A., which is entirely different."

The light turned green and Mother said, still speaking sharply, "We'll discuss the situation further. Get in."

"No, thank you," Susan said coolly. "I have things to do." A ride was tempting, tired as her arms were, but if she gave in now she was done for.

The car behind the Volks honked with annoyance and Mother drove on. Going to the grocery store, Susan guessed as she walked on down the road.

As Susan approached Antique Row she saw Mrs. Gaffney standing with her back to her on a chair in front of the shop. The old woman was trying to put up the faded sign that vandals or the wind had knocked down during the night.

Without turning around Mrs. Gaffney called out, "Good morning, Susan."

So witches did have eyes in the backs of their heads—a

disturbing thought. Susan's foot slipped off the curb, and as she caught her balance Sereena leaped out of her arms, dashed across the street, ran under the chair, through the door of the shop, and disappeared inside.

Susan ran after her as far as the door. She didn't dare go farther, not into a witch's den. But the cat was in there.

Her heart pounding, Susan walked into the shop. Mrs. Gaffney stepped heavily down from the chair, set it out of the way under the window, then followed Susan in, shutting the door behind her.

9

Gaffney's
Antique Shop

THE SHOP was dark and spooky, with furniture everywhere, even blocking the window so hardly any light could come in.

Susan wished she were safe at home, not in this dreadful place. "Here kitty, kitty, kitty," she called timidly, looking every which way, her heart thumping loud enough to hear.

"Don't worry about your cat," Mrs. Gaffney's voice said from the shadows behind her. "Both the front door and the back are shut. She can't escape."

Susan couldn't escape either and the air smelled moldy and Mrs. Gaffney was too close.

"Let me out of here," she cried. Turning toward the front door, whirling around fast, she bumped into a small oval mahogany table. Something fell to the floor and broke into pieces, one landing on her shoe.

"Oh, dear," said Mrs. Gaffney, "my Lowestoft teapot."

In a panic Susan ran to the door, grabbed the knob, turned it and pulled with both hands. It wouldn't open, locked on purpose to keep her a prisoner.

She screamed in fright, "Let me out of here!"

"Not until you calm down," said Mrs. Gaffney, grabbing her firmly by the shoulders.

Susan struggled frantically, beating the air with both hands. "No, no, let go of me, please let go of me." But she could not get away from the strong grip. She closed her eyes and held her breath, expecting to be changed into a frog the next moment.

She wasn't. After a long pause during which nothing happened at all, she opened her eyes again and said to bolster her courage, "Anyway, being a frog wouldn't be too bad. I like frogs."

"Frog? What in the world are you talking about?" Mrs. Gaffney asked.

Susan didn't answer right away. She waited, tense, until Mrs. Gaffney let go of her shoulders, then said, "My mother says there is no such thing as a witch. Other people say you are one." She looked straight into the old woman's eyes, as yellow as Sereena's and almost as inscrutable. "You are, aren't you?"

"Certainly not," was the indignant reply. "I am an old woman trying to earn my own living, that's all. Not easy to do these days, I can tell you. If business doesn't soon improve I'll be forced to give up and go live with my son in Philadelphia."

"Don't you like him?" Susan asked and Mrs. Gaffney said she did very much, too much to be a burden on him. She reached out and poked Susan in the ribs, adding, "If you can pay your own way, you're free and independent. If you can't, it's just too bad and don't you forget it."

"I won't," Susan told her and backed out of poking distance.

Now Mrs. Gaffney took a flowered lamp shade off of the red sofa and put it in the blue Canton platter on the table nearby. Then she sat down and patted a place beside her saying, "Sit here and tell me about your cat. I like cats. Years ago I had one."

"You do? You did?"

Mrs. Gaffney nodded. "He was killed on the road right in front of the shop, truck ran over him. Sit down, I'm not going to bite you. I want to hear about you and your cat."

"I'd feel better about things if the door were unlocked— not open so Sereena can get out, just unlocked so I can."

"The door is not locked. It's warped and sticks sometimes."

Susan, still wary, sat on the edge of the sofa, ready to bolt. Then, after swallowing twice, she told the cat's story, beginning with Trunko and buying him at the Flea Market with borrowed money. Mrs. Gaffney laughed an un-witch laugh when Hugo came into the plot. At the part when Mother said Sereena could not stay, she was sympathetic both ways, saying she knew it was hard for Susan to give up the cat and equally hard for Mother to say no.

Susan thought about that for a while before she said, "I still think Mother will give in and let me keep Sereena. She just needs time to get used to the idea. The way I figure it, if Sereena stayed away from our house at somebody else's for a few weeks, Mother would miss her. I'd visit her myself, of course."

She frowned, flinging out both arms as she said, "The trouble is nobody will keep her for me. I hate Joyce Gibbs. She's my friend, but she's mean."

Quickly Susan changed the subject to money. "Could I please pay you what I owe you next Saturday instead of to-day as I said I would? With the future uncertain, I may need it. I have it in my pocketbook at home in case you say no."

Mrs. Gaffney laughed again and said any time was all right with her. Then she pointed to a sign hanging on the kitchen door. "Speaking of money, Susan, read that."

Susan squinted to get a better look and read aloud: *If You Break It, You Have Bought It.* She covered her mouth with both hands for a second before exclaiming, "The teapot! I have to pay for it. How much?"

"Thirty-five dollars," was the alarming reply.

"Thirty-five *dollars!*" Susan jumped to her feet, almost adding a china pig to her already enormous bill.

"Lowestoft is hard to find these days and the teapot was in perfect condition," Mrs. Gaffney said.

Susan stooped and began picking up the pieces, counting, "five, six, seven. Do you suppose——" No, the teapot could never be mended. Thirty-five dollars and twenty-five cents; she'd be in debt the rest of her life.

"Ssssh. Listen," whispered Mrs. Gaffney. "She's over there in the corner."

Susan's eyes, accustomed to the dim light by now, saw a dollhouse about three feet high and four feet long, a marvelous Victorian house with a pointed roof. Something was in it, something alive and gray.

"You stand on this side, Mrs. Gaffney, to block her off while I sneak up on her from the other side."

"You'll never catch a cat that way," said Mrs. Gaffney, heading for the kitchen. A few minutes later she returned with a bowl of milk. Setting it on the floor beside the dollhouse door she said, "We'll lure her out of hiding, let her come to us." And tapping the bowl lightly, she added, "French Haviland, fragile and expensive enough to suit the most fastidious cat."

Straightening up with difficulty, she went on. "Speaking of cats, Susan, yours may stay here with me for a few days."

Susan had to think. This was too serious a decision to

make in haste. She herself would rather die than spend a night in this dirty, dusty, smelly shop but a cat might like it — mice, hiding places, and all. And even if Mrs. Gaffney were a witch, it wouldn't matter to a cat because witches and cats were always in cahoots, weren't they?

With Sereena close by, Susan could stop in to see her twice a day, maybe three times. She could feed her, pet her, take her for walks, hold her on her lap for hours at a time. The more Susan thought about Mrs. Gaffney's offer, the better she liked the idea.

"I thank you very much, Mrs. Gaffney," she said, "and Sereena thanks you. I'll pay her board, of course, and speaking of money could I work off some of my debt? Sweep the floor, dust things, paint and mend and maybe even help sell things if anybody should come to buy?"

"You'd work for a witch?" asked Mrs. Gaffney, looking too much like one for comfort.

"I'd do anything for Sereena, almost," Susan told her. "Besides I'm not as scared of you as I was. And you want to know something?"

Mrs. Gaffney nodded and Susan said, giving her a powerful look in the eye, "I'm a magician, myself. I can tell about things. Want me to tell you about this sofa we're sitting on?"

Mrs. Gaffney did, so Susan placed her hands palms down on the red velvet cushions and began in a high-pitched, storytelling voice. "Once upon a time there lived a beautiful widow who had three beautiful children. No, two, a boy and a girl. They did not have enough food, almost but not quite enough, and they didn't have enough money to buy more, either. The only valuable thing the beautiful widow owned was a handsome red velvet sofa. This one."

Rap, rap, rap!

Somebody was at the door, shaking the knob and calling, "Anybody here?"

"Customers," said Susan, getting to her feet. "Let them in and I'll go right to work and sell them something. Okay?"

Mrs. Gaffney hurried to the door and jerked it open. In came two well-dressed women, one tall, one short. To Susan's distress the tall one announced that they were just looking, not buying today.

Mrs. Gaffney told them to enjoy themselves and disappeared into the kitchen. Susan, determined to make a sale, followed the two women around the shop, saying look at this pitcher, see how pretty the lamp is, don't miss the desk. No sale. And then her luck changed. Not entirely her luck, more Sereena's.

The women were about to leave when the short one who was nosing around at the back of the shop called to the one by the door, "Wait, Edith. Come here and look at the cat's dish."

Cat's dish?

Susan beat Edith to it, and there was Sereena lapping milk

out of the French Haviland bowl with her adorable pink tongue.

"It is a beautiful bowl, Clara," Edith said. Turning to Mrs. Gaffney, who was standing in the kitchen doorway, she asked, "How much for the cat's dish?"

Then and there Sereena sold her dish, seventeen dollars plus tax. Susan wanted to pounce on Sereena and congratulate her with hugs, but the cat stalked away to a new hiding place before she could.

"Wasn't it wonderful, Mrs. Gaffney?" Susan asked as soon as the shop door closed behind the customers.

Mrs. Gaffney said it was indeed, that Sereena had earned her board and keep for at least a week and had paid off the twenty-five cent debt in full.

Susan ran home to tell Mother the news, not about owing for the broken teapot, just the good news.

What a comedown. Mother was not impressed. While making Susan a ham sandwich to tide her over until supper, she said having Mrs. Gaffney keep the cat for a week or two would merely postpone the issue — that a permanent home was the point.

In spite of being discouraged, Susan enjoyed the sandwich.

Then Mother made things more discouraging. "There's another thing, Susan. I do not want you hanging around the antique shop for hours at a time. Not that I have anything against Mrs. Gaffney. I just don't think a shop is the place for children." After a thick silence she added, "You are getting entirely too free and easy."

Chewing the last of the sandwich, Susan glared at her mother's back, watching her elbows as she washed the ham platter. She was not going to get married when she grew up. And if she did, she would not let her husband go away, and she would not have any children. If she did, she'd let them have all the cats they wanted and she'd let them run free and easy.

She pushed back her chair, drank the last of her milk, wiped her mouth on the back of her hand, wiped her hand on her skirt, and went up to her room. It was empty without Sereena and Trunko. She sat on the edge of the pink bed and folded her hands in her lap, feeling very sorry for herself. Dad gone, white elephant gone, cat practically gone. People can't keep on losing what they care about most, can they?

10

Gone But
Not Forgotten

BEING SORRY for yourself gets boring in no time, and yet
Susan couldn't seem to snap out of it. Maybe Mike could
help. After supper she walked down the hall and tapped on
his door, the one with the yellow sign on it in large black
letters: *SANCTUM SANCTORUM.*

"What now, Brown Cow?" Mike asked, opening the
door. It was so corny Susan almost didn't go in, and in two
seconds she was sorry she had. He was no help at all, only
halfway listened, chinning himself on the bar across the
top of the doorway the whole time she was talking.

When she stopped he dropped down, landed on her toes,
and without even apologizing said, "You think you have
troubles, what about *me?* I've got a chemistry test at nine
A.M. Monday." So selfish, and she'd counted on him because
up till then he'd been so nice about Sereena.

She left at once. There was no use saying any more to any-body who would compare a live cat with a dead test. Hugo Scott wouldn't. At least she didn't think he would, and right after supper she got the chance to find out.

Hugo drove up and stopped in front of the house, his car packed full of football players. He honked and they all yelled for Mike who was taking a shower. To speed things Hugo came into the house and called again, "Get a move on, Prescott, we haven't got all night!" Before he could get out the door Susan waylaid him and told him the news about Sereena.

He listened and was sympathetic. "Fight on. Full speed ahead. Don't give up, Susan," he said. And as he and Mike were going out the door he added over his shoulder, "In any battle, Susan, your greatest strength is the weakness of the enemy. Right, Prescott?"

"Right." The door banged shut and the boys were gone.

Susan stood still in the hall, thinking. Mother didn't have any weaknesses. As soon as she thought that, she wished she hadn't. It was okay to consider Joyce Gibbs the enemy, but not Mother who fed, clothed, loved, and worried about you three hundred and sixty-five days a year.

Feeling guilty and ashamed, she shouted, "Mo—ther, want to play gin rummy?" Mother liked games and Susan did too.

"Fine, dear," Mother answered from her study. "Set up

the card table and get out the cards. I'll be right down."

They played until nearly ten o'clock and Mother won every single game. Dad should be home, Susan thought as she went up to bed. He could beat Mother once in a while. She remembered how those two would laugh when he did, lusty, grownup laughs that filled the house, making it sure and safe. That was years ago.

Mother had laughed twice tonight. Once when she ginned catching Susan without a card down, again when Susan caught her with a joker and two aces. It was fun to be with Mother, just the two of them, a warm, good feeling, the opposite of being on your own. Susan wished she could hold on to one and still have the other.

When Mother came up to bed she stopped at Susan's door and said, "Skip Sunday School tomorrow and go to see the cat early this once—only don't get in Mrs. Gaffney's way."

"Yes. Thank you, Mother. Good night."

Nine o'clock the next morning, wearing blue jeans, red checked shirt, tennis shoes, and Mike's outgrown baseball cap, Susan rapped on the antique shop door. She wasn't scared much this time. Still, a thrill of fear swept over her when the door creaked open and Mrs. Gaffney looked out.

"The shop doesn't open for business until ten," she said, yawning, showing where a tooth was missing on the top left side. "Oh, it's you, Susan. I didn't recognize you in that getup. Come in. I'm glad to see you, though I have bad news. Your cat's gone."

"Gone! When? Where did she go?"

Mrs. Gaffney explained that right after supper the evening before, a dealer stopped in on business, left the door ajar, and the cat had gone out.

"Did you actually see her go?" asked Susan, fighting to keep control of herself.

"No."

"Then she may be here still, hiding the way she did at first."

"I doubt it," Mrs. Gaffney said. "The milk I set out for her last night is still in the saucer and I haven't heard a sound."

Susan, emotions mounting, shook a stubby finger at the old woman. "I trusted you to take care of my cat and you didn't do it. Oh, I hate everybody!"

Mrs. Gaffney sat down in a rocking chair with a sagging

wicker seat, leaned forward, rested her head in her hand, and said sadly, "I don't blame you for hating me, Susan. Everything I try to do turns out wrong. I'm sorry for your sake and for my own. I liked that cat. She was company for me." She straightened and looked at Susan. "It isn't easy to live alone."

Susan dropped down on her knees beside Mrs. Gaffney and put her arms around her for a swift second. You touch a witch at your peril. Then she jumped up and headed for the door, saying, "I'll be back as soon as I find Sereena. Most likely she's at our house now waiting for me to let her in."

Sereena was not at the Prescotts'. She was not over at Bensons' or up at Amy's or at any other house close by, and nobody had seen her. Nobody along Falls Road had seen her, either, from Bird Lane down to the bridge. Susan rapped on door after door to ask.

Sereena could be out of sight up a tree somewhere or lying dead, run over by a car or killed by a dog. Or maybe somebody had cat-napped her, though that was not likely after the way she had been roaming the street for nobody knew how long before Susan got her.

Mother resorted to the police when she was in what she called "dire straits." Right now was dire for Susan, but she didn't have a dime in her pocket and you can't even dial O for operator without one.

Not knowing what else to do, Susan went home for comfort.

She did not get it. Mike accused her of being careless with Hugo's gift and anybody could tell at a glance that Mother hoped for the worst. However, under pressure Mother telephoned the police, the S.P.C.A., and the Humane Society to report a missing cat — long, low, thin, gray, not young, with yellow eyes.

Still sitting by the phone in the hall, Mother said to Susan, "At least you won't have to hang around that antique shop anymore."

Susan was quick to say, "Yes I do. I don't want to with Sereena not there, but I have to. I owe Mrs. Gaffney a lot of money and I'm going to pay it back by sweeping out the shop, dusting, mending — things like that."

"How much money do you owe, Susan?" Mother asked sharply. "And why in the world do you owe her anything?"

Hesitantly Susan explained.

"Thirty-five dollars for one teapot!" exclaimed Mother.

"Lowestoft," declared Susan in a knowing tone of voice and Mike said, "Wow."

After a moment of reflection, Mother reached over and took Susan's hand, saying, "Don't worry, dear. It was an accident. I'll write Mrs. Gaffney a check."

Standing as tall as she could, Susan said formally, "No

thank you. No matter what, accident or not, the responsibility is mine."

Mother gave her a long look. "Good for you," she said.

After a pause Susan said, "Speaking of responsibility, Sereena is a responsible cat. Before she disappeared she sold a French Haviland milk dish for seventeen dollars. Mrs. Gaffney said she earned enough to pay her board and keep for two weeks and more—that is, if she comes back, and I'm sure she will because she has to."

"No plain ordinary cat ever sold anything and you know it," Mike told her, flipping his hair back so he could see better.

That was a new idea, and a good one, Susan thought. Maybe Sereena wasn't an ordinary cat. Maybe she was a magic cat. If so, she might appear at any moment as mysteriously as she had disappeared.

Susan went to the door and called once more, "Here kitty, kitty, kitty."

Across the lane in the woods some stupid bird or something answered, "Peep, peep." Nothing else, enough to drive you mad.

Eyes closed, fingers crossed for good luck, Susan tried some magic of her own. It didn't work. Nothing came to her except hope.

After school tomorrow she'd start to work at Gaffney's,

not today. A delicious smell came from the kitchen down the hall straight to Susan's nose.

"Mother, what's for lunch? I'm starved."

"Baked potatoes, hamburgers, and tossed salad."

Marvelous. Would Sereena have any lunch at all? Susan didn't know, but she was pretty sure the cat, ordinary or magic, was alive somewhere. She had to be.

11

Sereena Salescat

AT SCHOOL Monday morning Susan, headed down the hall to her room, passed Joyce Gibbs, headed up the hall to her room. They stopped long enough for Joyce to ask the latest cat news and Susan to tell it. By recess, practically everybody in the whole school knew that Sereena had disappeared from Gaffney's antique shop. By lunch time, rumors were flying.

A boy in the fifth grade said he bet anything Mrs. Gaffney had put a spell on the cat to make it disappear into nothing. And a girl in Joyce's class said Mrs. Gaffney's own cat had disappeared into nothing, somebody had told her so, she'd forgotten who. Susan tried to tell her Mrs. Gaffney's cat had been run over but the girl wouldn't even listen.

Evelyn Belt, who sat behind Susan, claimed Mrs. Gaffney's cat had been changed into a bat and she wouldn't be a bit surprised if Sereena was one by now too.

Tom Baily, a sixth grader, said witches make a potent brew out of stewed cat and a couple of other things.

Selma Varn, a seventh grader who played the violin at nearly all assemblies, said Mrs. Gaffney might have sold Susan's cat to a maker of violins, adding—and she didn't need to—"strings are made out of catgut, you know."

Susan didn't swallow the rumors; nevertheless, they made her feel uneasy. She didn't stop at Gaffney's that day as planned.

The next day, things got worse. One of the boys in Joyce's class said that one time when he was in the antique shop with his father, something cooking in the back room in a big rusty pot smelled very much like cat soup.

Susan knew he was just making that up, and said so. Still, the place had smelled strange the last time she was there . . .

Thursday, a dozen or so kids from school trooped up Falls Road as far as Mrs. Gaffney's and hung around out in front of the shop for a half hour, making goofy noises and throwing pebbles up onto the roof. Susan wasn't with them. She and Amy watched and listened from the hump of Bird Hill. They saw a police car come cruising along and then the kids scrammed.

Friday, one of the boys who'd been in the gang on Thursday told Susan he thought he'd seen a gray cat looking out the shop window. Well, dirty as that window was, anybody could imagine he'd seen almost anything he wanted to see.

It all added up to confusion for Susan. Friday during supper she told Mother, "I've changed my mind about the check for thirty-five dollars. I'll take it."

Mike was out to supper and Susan was glad because Mother's "Very well" and her expression packed a wallop. Such a wallop in fact that Susan couldn't get to sleep that night.

Finally she called, "Mother, no check. I've changed my mind back again, and this is final. I'm starting to work at Mrs. Gaffney's tomorrow for absolutely sure, and I'm going to work the whole weekend."

"I'm glad, Susan," Mother said, coming up the stairs. "You can work in the morning, but plan to be home in the afternoon. Your father is in town on business and will stop out to see you children either tomorrow afternoon or some time on Sunday."

"That's good news," Susan said. It was. She hadn't seen Dad for . . . let's see . . . eight months last Tuesday.

Susan lay back down. Now if she'd only hear some word about Sereena. At least she knew where Trunko was. Work tomorrow. Cats and bats, and bats and cats, and smells and witches. Those rumors were stupid. Anyhow, if Mrs. Gaffney really was a witch, she was not cruel. Sleep came at last and swiftly it was morning.

Susan went to work early and found Mrs. Gaffney sitting outdoors on a wooden chair beside the shop step, not doing anything at all, just sitting there huddled in a black shawl over her heavy gray sweater.

"Any news of your cat?" the old woman asked.

Susan shook her head no. Mrs. Gaffney said a friend of hers had a cat that stayed away nearly a year and came back. Inspired by that, Susan felt like working. "Now for the debt," she said, rubbing her hands together. "How much per hour am I worth?"

"I'll have to wait and see," Mrs. Gaffney said, getting to her feet. "How about fifty cents an hour as a starter, with a chance of a raise later?"

"That's fair," Susan said, taking a three by two notebook out of the patch pocket of her jeans and a stub of a pencil from her shirt pocket. She licked the point of the pencil and wrote, foot on step, book on knee, "Fifty goes into thirty-five seven times—I mean seventy. Seventy hours of work. Ten days of seven hours a day, or twenty days of three and a half hours."

"I'll take your word for it," Mrs. Gaffney said as she went into the shop. Susan followed, sniffing. Although those cat rumors weren't true, it was easy to see how some of them got started.

"First, let's wash the window. Want to?" suggested Susan.

Mrs. Gaffney did, but there were problems. They couldn't get to the window until they moved the bookcase, and it wouldn't budge with the three bottom shelves full of books and the two top ones loaded with dishes. Besides, even if the bookcase would budge, where would it go? A table blocked one side and a china closet the other.

Susan began by stacking books on the floor. "If you have a dustpan and a broom, and a basin of water and a rag, I could use them."

Mrs. Gaffney mosied out into the kitchen and returned, basin in hand, rag draped over an arm, broom under one arm, dustpan under the other. Susan called to her, "I do think Sereena is alive, don't you? I mean, I'd feel it if she weren't, wouldn't I?"

Mrs. Gaffney said gloomily that it was best not to count on feelings, she'd found them to be unreliable.

Ignoring that, Susan swept vigorously, filling the air, her hair, and her clothes full of dust. She'd never worked so hard. Then she stacked more books, stopping to read two chapters of *Dotty Dimple,* the pages dry and brown as fall leaves.

Piling dishes on the edge of the table was fun, they were so pretty. One with tiny blue flowers around the edge was her favorite, and Mrs. Gaffney said she could have it. Maybe she'd keep it on her bureau top for pins and things. Better still, she'd give it to Mother to take the place of her half of Trunko. She'd wait and see. Something else very special might turn up. An antique shop was like an enormous Christmas stocking, it really was.

Empty, the bookcase still wouldn't move much, only five inches. But five inches of light was better than none, especially since Mrs. Gaffney could reach back there now with her long arm to wash the window.

Susan turned next to the dollhouse. It was so charming it almost made her forget Sereena. Not quite, though. Squatting in front of the old-fashioned house with its carved porch rail, gingerbread window trim, and more trim running up and down the peak roof, Susan thought about the girl who owned it years ago when it was new. She ran her fingers over the faded wallpaper in the living room, empty now except for spider webs. Six rooms, all empty, three upstairs, three down.

"It was part of the Barr estate," Mrs. Gaffney said, standing close behind Susan, so close it gave her the creeps. "The highboy came from there too, and the Chippendale table, the dining room chairs, and those two trunks." She leaned heavily on Susan's shoulder with one hand, the other pointing toward the far corner of the shop. "Look in that trunk, the small leather one with the quilt across it. I have a notion you might find a chair or a table from the dollhouse in it."

Susan scrambled to her feet and made her way toward the trunk. As she was climbing over a low table, there was a rap, rap, rap, at the door.

"Come in. Push the door hard, it's not locked," Mrs.

Gaffney called out in her strong voice.

A young man with a beard and a lot of hair poked his head in and asked, "How much for the cat's chair?"

The cat's chair!

In her haste, Susan upset an umbrella stand full of canes, but it was brass and didn't break. Then she stepped right in a washtub full of tin lids, creating a terrible racket, before she finally made it to the door.

There on Mrs. Gaffney's straight back chair out front sat Sereena — back straight too, tail hanging over the edge of the seat.

"Darling!" Susan exclaimed, swooping down upon her beloved cat.

Mrs. Gaffney was pleased, but she didn't forget the business at hand. "The chair is eight dollars," she told the young man. "One back rung is missing."

"Sold." The man paid in cash, picked up the chair, put it in the back of his car, and drove away.

By this time Sereena was grooming herself on the red sofa, left hind leg high in the air.

Admiring her, Susan said, "Selling the Haviland dish might have happened to any cat. Selling a dish *and* a chair is something else. Sereena is definitely not a plain ordinary cat. She is a magic salescat."

Mrs. Gaffney agreed, looking extremely witchy as she pocketed the young man's money.

Susan beamed. Sereena had come home at last. No, she hadn't. Home was number 5 Bird Lane. Sereena had come back to Gaffney's antique shop—and the more Susan thought about that, the less she liked it.

Look at Mrs. Gaffney now, stroking the cat. Sereena, the fickle thing, stretched out flat on the sofa like the Queen of Sheba on a barge and soaked up the petting. It was enough to make you die then and there of jealousy. You heap all your love on a cat, and you get back the other side of nothing.

This was a new way of losing, having what you love choose someone else. Susan frowned, feeling terrible. Jealousy was wicked, went deep, and hurt. Dad had done the same thing. How could Mother go on keeping house, cooking, working, paying bills? Well, Dad did pay some of the bills, those the court made him pay.

Susan suddenly hated Sereena, Mrs. Gaffney, Dad, *and* Mother, all of them at once, and each separately for a different reason. And all the magic in the world couldn't cure it. Joyce had told her once that she should find out what kind of a person she was. Well, Susan knew what kind she was right now—one who loved madly and hated just as madly. More maybe.

"Why the scowl, Susan?" Mrs. Gaffney asked. "Aren't you glad the cat came back to us, safe and sound? Wait, someone is at the door."

It was Joyce of all people. Poking her head through the half-open door, she called, "Yoo-hoo, Susan. Oh, there you are. Hello, Mrs. Gaffney."

Then, not giving Susan a chance to say beans, Joyce rattled on a mile a minute about how she'd gotten her mother to drive her to Susan's house to find out the latest news about the cat episode. Mrs. Prescott had told her Susan was at Gaffney's, so here she was and what was happening?

Susan bristled. It was just like Joyce to refer to Sereena's dramatic, mysterious disappearance as the cat episode. That girl couldn't say how-do without making you mad. By way of an answer, Susan motioned toward the red sofa.

Joyce crossed the floor slowly, being careful not to let the hem of her skirt touch anything, and leaned over the back of the sofa. "So there she is, alive after all, and where she belongs if you ask me."

Another dig. Before Susan had a chance to snap back at her, Joyce spied the dollhouse and sang out, "It's bea-u-ti-ful, simply bea-u-ti-ful! I must have it. How much is it, Mrs. Gaffney?"

In a bolt Susan knew she wanted the dollhouse herself. She held her breath and then sighed aloud when Mrs. Gaffney said, "It is not for sale at the moment. I haven't had it appraised yet, so I can't quote a price."

"I see," said Joyce. "Well, let me know as soon as you do know. My name is in the telephone book—Joyce Gibbs.

I have my own phone."

She looked around and added, "This place could be really marvelous, Mrs. Gaffney, if you fixed it up and got in more dollhouses and things like that."

A car horn sounded outside and Joyce said, "That's my mother blowing for me. I've got to run. Oh, Susan, I almost forgot to tell you. Your mother says to come right home. Bye now. Bye, Mrs. Gaffney. Don't forget to call me about the dollhouse. See you later!"

Bang, Joyce was gone.

"What time is it?" asked Susan.

"Twelve-thirty," Mrs. Gaffney said. "You worked so hard that I'm giving you a ten cent an hour raise and an extra dollar, your commission on the cat's chair sale. How does that strike you?"

"Fine. Thank you. Four hours of work at sixty cents an hour comes to two dollars and forty cents. That plus a dollar makes three-forty. And that from thirty-five dollars—let's see." Susan leaned over and did the subtraction with her finger in the dust on the table top. "I still owe you $31.60. Right?"

Mrs. Gaffney nodded and Susan left the shop in a rush. Two seconds later she came back and said, "I'm glad you didn't sell Joyce the dollhouse. For one thing, she gets every-thing she wants. Besides, I want it myself. After I pay off the thirty-one sixty, couldn't I buy the dollhouse on the installment plan?"

Mrs. Gaffney nodded again and Susan left a second time. A second later she was back again. This time she asked, "How much? I know you don't know for sure, but take a guess. Ten dollars?"

"More than that."

"Fifteen?"

"More."

"Twenty-five?"

"Give or take five or ten dollars, twenty-five should cover it."

"Then it's settled. Joyce doesn't get it ever?"

Mrs. Gaffney nodded once more and Susan left for good this time, pulling the obstinate door shut behind her.

She raced home. Sereena alive, the dollhouse in the offing, her debt beginning to dwindle, and Dad coming. It was turning out to be a very good day.

12

Thick as Thieves

"SEREENA'S BACK at the antique shop and she's okay,"
Susan announced in a loud voice as she came into the house.

"I'm glad for your sake, dear," Mother said, coming to the
kitchen door, apron on, flour on her hands.

"What about for *her* sake?" Susan asked and Mother
went back into the kitchen, saying, "Let's not get into another cat hassle. I said I was glad and I am. Go take a bath
and change your clothes. If your father does come today, he's
apt to come early. He wrote that he has to go to a business
dinner at six-thirty."

Susan skipped steps as she went upstairs. So as usual Dad
wasn't coming just to see the family. As usual there was another reason too. Everything was mixed, never straight this
or that. Well, even so, once he got home he might decide to
stay. He could make up his mind to all of a sudden. That's

the way he left, so why shouldn't he come back the same way? She filled the tub full, yanked off her clothes, and hopped in, head and all. Her hair was as dirty as the rest of her.

What to put on? The pink dress was the prettiest, but green was Dad's favorite color. She'd wear the green jumper, the new white blouse, and her patent leather shoes. She dressed carefully, taking time to brush and brush her hair until it was almost dry. Then she walked downstairs sedately and presented herself to Mother in the kitchen.

"How do I look?" she asked, twirling around on her toes.

"Beautiful," Mother said, the word all in one piece, not the silly way Joyce said it.

Lunch was soon over. Now if Dad would only hurry up and get there.

Waiting really was tiring. Two o'clock, three, not a sign of him. At a quarter of four Susan stopped looking out the front window and went upstairs to her room. She got out a notebook, the one she kept for special things, and jotted on a fresh page: $25.00 — one dollhouse. On another page she wrote thirty-five dollars minus three-forty equals thirty-one sixty.

Then she made a collar for Sereena out of an outgrown tan leather belt, cut it shorter, and printed on it: SEREENA PRESCOTT, 5 BIRD LANE. She hoped the ink was water-proof. If it wasn't it wouldn't matter much, though, because cared-for cats seldom went out in the rain.

Still no Dad.

Five-thirty the telephone rang—Dad to say he was sorry he couldn't make it, a meeting lasted longer than he'd expected. He'd do his best to stop in tomorrow.

He didn't come Sunday, either. Susan and Mike hung around home all day long, dressed up, restless and edgy as caged hyenas. During supper Susan said, "Dad cost me plenty—three hours Saturday and six hours Sunday, maybe more, not to mention being away from my cat all that time. And those two, Mrs. Gaffney and Sereena, are thick as thieves."

The phrase, thick as thieves, conjured up a dramatic scene in Susan's head, a forest of trees and behind each tree a thief that looked like a blend of Dad, Mrs. Gaffney, and Sereena —with whiskers and a long tail. Susan was so absorbed in the fantasy she missed hearing the list of important engagements Mike had broken to stay home.

She did hear her mother say with a tight lip, "Your father did not say he would come, only that he would *try* to."

"Big deal," Mike said and Susan made a face, a sort of squashed-out grin. Anyway, the food was good.

After supper, while Susan was washing the dishes (it was her turn), she told Mother all about the dollhouse, and how Joyce Gibbs wanted it, and she wanted it also. To her surprise Mother said she'd always wanted a dollhouse herself and never had one.

Susan looked around at Mother, wiping dishes. Even using magic she couldn't figure why anybody who liked white elephants and dollhouses didn't like cats. There was no telling about people.

As Susan went upstairs to do her homework, Mother called after her, "In the letter I got from your father he said if he didn't get out to see you children this weekend, to expect him weekend after next."

"Big deal." Susan repeated Mike's words under her breath so Mother couldn't hear. In the dark hall her thoughts switched quickly from Dad to Sereena and Mrs. Gaffney. Thick as thieves.

She was glad when the light in her room clicked on. Now to write a story for English class tomorrow. What about? Let's see. She undressed, put on her favorite nightgown, pink with sprigs of flowers in all directions, sat down at her desk, curled bare toes around the chair rung, and wrote at the top of a fresh piece of composition paper *Thick as Thieves*.

This was fun. She wrote a wild tale about a bunch of cat thieves. Down the hall in her study Mother was writing too, typing away. Their lights went out about the same time and Mike's not much later. Susan liked the family in one piece, what there was of it.

On Monday Mother went to Washington to do some research on trends in education. Mrs. Benson picked up Susan right after school and wouldn't let her stay at Mrs. Gaffney's longer than the five minutes it took to put the new collar on Sereena. It fit, gave the cat a neat finished look, and told the world who she was and where she belonged, something Susan did not want Mrs. Gaffney to forget.

Tuesday, because of a teacher's meeting, school closed at noon, giving Susan a lot of time for work. By twelve forty-five she was at the antique shop trying to open the small leather trunk.

"See if one of these will fit," Mrs. Gaffney said, producing a key ring with what looked like half a million keys on it, most of them rusty.

Susan tried twenty-seven keys. The twenty-eighth fit. She turned it in the lock and lifted the lid. Out came a strange odor of ghosts and old things that had been locked up for a long, long time. On the top was a small boat-shaped black hat with a fluffy feather drooping down on the side. Susan put it on and at once felt like someone from long ago. Leaving it on, she lifted out a lacy shawl, delicate as a spider web, once white, now yellow and much too fragile to wear.

She laid the shawl aside and picked up a purple dress with a full skirt and such a tiny waist. Underneath it was a little jewel box. Susan opened the lid and exclaimed, "Look what

I found, Mrs. Gaffney. A marvelous ring. It's too big for my finger but I'll bet it would fit my mother."

"It's yours. You may have it," Mrs. Gaffney said. "Pure genuine imitation ruby, imitation gold, and imitation pearls."

"Even so, it is beautiful," Susan told her. "Thank you very much. I love it and Mother will, too." She put it on her thumb and admired it, head on the side, hat nearly falling off. "See how it sparkles?"

Mrs. Gaffney, sitting in the rocker again with Sereena on her lap again, wasn't listening. Those two. Turning back to the trunk, Susan untied a faded blue ribbon that was tied around an old suit box. "Hey," she sang out so loud Sereena bolted, "I found the doll furniture! Come look, there's lots of it."

She sat back on her heels and, with Mrs. Gaffney leaning over her shoulder, examined piece after piece of miniature furniture. It was perfect in every detail: dining room table —Chippendale so Mrs. Gaffney said—six Chippendale chairs to match, a four-poster bed, bureau, crib, kitchen stove, cupboard full of tiny pots and pans. And best of all, wrapped in blue tissue paper, was the family of dolls: mother in a full skirt, dark hair close to her head; father wearing a black suit, white shirt with a high collar, and a mustache that drooped at the ends; a boy in kneepants; a

baby; a nurse with white apron and cap; and last of all a plump pug dog.

Susan almost burst. "All this couldn't be included in the house price," she said, looking up at Mrs. Gaffney. "How much more would it be do you suppose — ten dollars?"

"That should cover it," was the answer. "Fifteen perhaps."

Susan couldn't wait to furnish her house. Still wearing the hat, she wiped out the dollhouse inside and out with a damp cloth, dried it, mended the roof and tacked down the loose porch rail. Then with Sereena sitting close by watching she arranged things in the upstairs rooms saying, "When I get time I'll weave a rug or two, make curtains, pillows, and blankets. That will be fun."

As she put the dining room table in place the shop door opened and in came Joyce and her mother. Mrs. Gibbs was a handsome woman, president of the P.T.A., head of the Women's Council at St. John's Church, a real go-getter like Joyce and she looked like her also, only bigger and older. And she was almost as bossy.

"We came to see the — " Joyce stopped short and burst out laughing. "You slay me in that hat, Susan. Where did you get it?"

Before Susan could say a word, Joyce dropped to her knees in front of the dollhouse, squealing, "It's *furnished!*

How positively marvelous. Look, Mother, the house is divine and the furniture is super, the best I've even seen except at the Smithsonian."

Sereena vanished under the Hepplewhite lowboy. Mrs. Gibbs, after greeting Mrs. Gaffney, leaned over, examined the dollhouse critically, then asked if it had been appraised. Upon being told it had not, she asked if she might call an appraiser, a friend of hers who was interested in rare antiques.

Mrs. Gaffney said she'd be glad to have someone see it as she was curious herself and would like to know its value. However, she thought it only fair to tell Mrs. Gibbs that the dollhouse had already been sold.

At that Joyce flew into a rage. She stamped her foot and shouted at Mrs. Gaffney rudely, "You *knew* I wanted it. I told you to call me and you didn't." Pouting, she pulled at her mother's sleeve saying, "Find out who bought it and offer him twice what he paid for it, three times if he won't take twice."

"A her bought it or is about to," Susan said, "Me."

"*YOU!*"

Joyce glared at Susan who said, "Yes, and I won't give it up for a million dollars."

"It isn't fair," Joyce declared in a loud voice. "I said I wanted it first. Besides that, I want it much more than you do, Susan, and I'm going to get it too. You just wait. Somehow that dollhouse is going to be mine. Come on, Mother, let's get out of here."

Mrs. Gibbs apologized to Mrs. Gaffney for her daughter's outburst. Then the two of them left the shop, Joyce slamming the door so forcefully after them that it didn't stick. As soon as the dust settled, Susan turned to Mrs. Gaffney, "She couldn't get it, could she? I mean you gave me your word and I know you'd never go back on it."

"Thank you, Susan," the old woman said, stooping to pick up Sereena who had appeared again and was rubbing against her leg.

Susan sat down on a hump-top trunk, folded her arms, blew the drooping hat feather out of her eyes, and said, "That girl has the worst manners in the whole world, positively the worst."

Mrs. Gaffney didn't say anything, so after a long while Susan added, "She does not want the dollhouse more than I do, or as much really. I want it as much as I did Trunko and almost as much as I do Sereena."

Everything was still. Presently Susan heard the soft creak of the rocker, Mrs. Gaffney rocking slowly, leaning back, eyes closed, a peaceful expression on her wrinkled face, the cat asleep on her lap.

Jealousy tasted bitter on Susan's tongue. She wanted Mrs.

Gaffney and Sereena to be friends but she didn't want them to be an exclusive two, neither one needing her at all.

Well, Mother needed her, that's for sure. If it weren't for her and Mike, Mother wouldn't be Mother. She'd go home now and give her the ring and tell her about finding the dollhouse furniture and the doll family.

Imagine owning a furnished, lived-in dollhouse that Joyce Gibbs wanted a whole lot and couldn't get!

The rocking chair had stopped creaking. Susan looked over and saw both occupants asleep, one with her mouth open, the other with her tail encircling her body in a beautiful curve.

The cat problem was still far from solved, still on a temporary basis, which wasn't good. However, in the dollhouse the old dolls, awakened like Sleeping Beauties, were picking up the threads of their lives once again — and that was very good.

Susan took off the hat, set it on top of the blue lamp shade, put the imitation gold ring on her thumb, turned it three times to the right, three times to the left for good luck, then went home.

13

The Cat's Place

MOTHER LIKED the ring. She put it on and it fit so perfectly she couldn't get it off. On forever, Susan thought to herself, and for a second she saw in her mind's eye Mother old and gray as Mrs. Gaffney, rocking, her lap empty, the ring flashing on her lean finger.

Mother was interested in hearing about the dollhouse and furniture and dolls, very interested. She said she wanted to see them some day when she had time.

"Tomorrow?" Susan asked and Mother answered, "Not tomorrow. Another day soon."

That night Susan had a dream, at least she thought it was a dream. In it Mrs. Gaffney was sitting in the rocking chair with Sereena on her lap just the way she sat in the shop. Woman, cat, and rocker got smaller and smaller and smaller until they were dollhouse size and Susan was holding them in her hands. All at once somebody grabbed them from her and she woke up crying aloud, "No, no, they are mine, both of them are *mine!*"

Hearing the cry, Mother hurried into Susan's room, switched on the light, and said, "Everything is all right, dear. You were having a nightmare, that's all."

Susan sat straight up in bed, eyes round. "If it was a nightmare," she said, "it had a magic ending because now I know what to do about my cat and Mrs. Gaffney. I'll give the cat to Mrs. Gaffney and keep them both. Isn't that a marvelous solution to the whole situation?"

Without giving Mother a chance to say a word, Susan went on, "Before you turn out the light, would you tuck me in the way you used to? Sam and Octavia are on the floor." She remembered Trunko and felt a brief pang of loss.

Mother laughed as she picked up the toys and lined them up beside the rest of the family, putting Ted and Teddy in her arms. Then she brushed Susan's hair back off of her forehead with her hand, gently saying, "Sometimes my daughter is a grownup young woman, other times she is still a little girl."

Snuggling down under the covers, hugging the bears, Susan felt both ways at once. For at least ten minutes after the light was turned off she thought and thought about cat *and* witch belonging to her. That way nobody lost anything, everybody got pretty much what she wanted. Very good.

Soon it was morning and she couldn't wait to tell Mrs. Gaffney the news. She'd have to wait until after school, though, because Mother was in no mood to stop at the antique shop on the way.

The morning went by slowly, but not lunch hour. Joyce waylaid her at the cafeteria door. "Eat lunch with me," she said and led the way to the corner table by the window. She was so pleasant Susan suspected she was up to something, and she was.

"The appraiser is going to see the dollhouse today," Joyce announced. "And my mother says if he says it is really valuable she's going to call a lawyer to find out if there is any way we could get it legally."

Susan didn't say a word, she was too angry. She just ate her sandwich, ham on rye, her eyes snapping.

"After all," Joyce added, "it should be mine." Then she overstepped the bounds. "I've already decided that I'll call the grownup dolls Mr. and Mrs. Prince; the boy doll will be Caspar, the baby, Delores, and the French dog, Fifi."

Susan, furious, swallowed a rather large hunk of bread and said, "How dare you name my dolls! Of all the nerve." She narrowed her eyes, leaned close to Joyce's face, and said in a gritty tone, "For your information their names are Mr. and Mrs. Charles Ravenell Barr, of the Barr estate you know, Charles Ravenell Barr, Jr., baby Amy Louise, and the dog— who is definitely Chinese—is Chew-Chew, hyphenated.

And don't you forget it, Joyce Gibbs."

"What's going on over there at table five?" asked the gym teacher who was on duty that day.

"Nothing, Mr. Barnes," Joyce told him sweetly. "Susan Prescott and I are just playing."

"Fibber," hissed Susan. Joyce giggled, mayonnaise daubs at the corners of her mouth. "You are so funny when you're mad, Susan, a perfect scream really." She gave her a shove and added, "Say you don't hate me and I'll tell you a secret."

"What is it?"

"Say it."

"I will not. Tell me or I really will hate you."

"That means you don't. Well, say please and promise you won't tell a soul I told you."

"Please and I promise not to tell."

After purposely waiting an infuriatingly long time, Joyce said, "Your brother Mike is going to play first string football from now on."

"He is? How do you know? Are you sure?"

"I'm sure. Hugo Scott told his mother, she told my mother, and she told me. The reason it's a secret is Hugo wants to be the one to tell Mike just before the next game, surprise him. Don't you spill the beans and spoil things."

"I won't, but what about Pete Griffith? I thought he was next in line for first string."

"Pete's the whole point. He ran his Honda into a tree or

a telephone pole and broke his arm or his leg or something."

"That's too bad for him, though good for Mike," Susan said as the bell rang, ending the lunch hour. With much scraping of feet and pushing back of chairs the children streamed out of the cafeteria, Joyce last, quickly eating half a sandwich.

Susan walked down the hall to her room. The very idea of that girl naming her doll family and talking about bringing in a lawyer so she could get the dollhouse for herself. The secret about Mike was a plus, though.

After school Mother was on time, waiting out front impatiently, already late for a meeting, so she said. Would Susan please get in the car and stop dawdling? All right, she'd let her off at Gaffney's if she promised not to stay long. Mother told her to leave her books in the car and try not to get her school dress too dirty.

In no time Susan was opening the door of the antique shop, calling, "Mrs. Gaffney, where are you? I have some news to tell you."

Mrs. Gaffney, looking more disheveled than usual, came to the kitchen door, coffee cup in hand, not Haviland. "Oh, it's you," she said, "I thought from the racket it was the fire department."

Susan pushed a straight chair over near the old woman, saying, "Sit down and give me your full attention."

Mrs. Gaffney lowered herself onto the chair, sipping

coffee on the way down, saying between sips, "Fire away."

Susan squatted on the floor in front of her, back straight, arms folded. "You want to keep Sereena, don't you?" she said.

"If I weren't moving I'd like to."

"Moving? What do you mean moving? We've been all over that and decided to make a fresh start so you wouldn't have to move."

"I know, I know, Susan." She shook her head and went on, "But, sometimes I think it's too late to start again. So much needs doing around here. The shop roof leaks. The floor boards are weak. I can't fight alone any more."

"You won't be alone. That's what I'm about to tell you. I'll give Sereena to you to be yours forever and both of you will be mine forever. By magic you can do things like that. The idea came to me in a nightmare. Great, isn't it?"

"Sounds all right except the forever part. Nothing lasts forever, Susan."

"Oh, yes it does. Cats, people, and other living things don't. But what's between them does if it's special enough, and for sure what's between Sereena, you, and me is special."

"I'll take your word for it," Mrs. Gaffney said, leaning forward and patting Susan on the head as though she were a cat. "Thank you, child. To celebrate I'll cross off your old debt. All you owe me for now is the dollhouse and the furniture."

"And the dolls," Susan put in.

"And the dolls," repeated Mrs. Gaffney. "Speaking of the dolls, the appraiser was here this morning and he was quite taken by the mother doll."

"He was? That's good. What did he say about the house and the rest of the things?" Susan wanted to know.

"He took quite a number of photographs of the four-poster bed and the little dining room table and told me he'd get in touch with me in a day or two. He wanted to discuss the dollhouse with the director of the museum before stating its value. From the way he acted, though, my guess is you've got yourself a bargain."

"Great. Now for business," Susan said, rubbing her hands together. "First of all, we need a new sign out front. How about calling the shop *The Cat's Place* from now on."

"I like that. *The Cat's Place* it is," Mrs. Gaffney answered with a jerky nod and Susan was delighted. "I'll paint a board red, then as soon as it's dry I'll paint on the letters in black, and above them a side view of Sereena in gray, long tail, head up, plenty of whiskers. Black and gray against red will be pretty. Everybody will stop when they see the sign, they'll come in and buy things. Business will boom and the three of us will live happily ever after."

Mrs. Gaffney laughed, saying, "I believe you really are a magician, Susan. We'll give *The Cat's Place* a chance to prove it. I can always sell out if we fail."

"We won't fail," Susan declared. "A witch, a magician, and a magic salescat couldn't possibly fail."

She stood up and started for the door. "I've got to go now, but I'll be back as soon as I can. Goodby, Mrs. Gaffney. Take care of our cat. Where is she?" She glanced around the shop and spied Sereena watching the wood basket. "There she is. I bet she smells a mouse."

Susan turned again toward the old woman. "You're not a witch, not really, Mrs. Gaffney. I just said you were for fun."

Mrs. Gaffney raised one eyebrow and grinned at her with an extremely witchy grin.

"Oh, you," Susan said, "I don't know for sure what you are."

Mrs. Gaffney's grin changed to a hearty laugh and Susan ran out the door and all the way home without stopping.

14

The Bargain

DAYS FLEW BY fast and here it was Friday already. Mike had to stay home from school because he ached all over, had a sore throat, a drippy nose, and a temperature of a hundred and one. He drank gallons of water, gargled with warm salt water every fifteen minutes, and grouched.

Mother told him to keep his germs in his room but he kept coming to the door to yell in a frog voice, "I don't care what anybody says, I'm going to the football game tomorrow—even if they have to carry me out to the field on a stretcher."

Susan wished she could tell Mike the secret to cheer him up, but since she'd given her word not to, of course she couldn't. Instead she just told him to cheer up, which made him do the opposite.

After school Susan went to Amy's birthday party. It was

all right, though to a mature girl in the antique business some of the games seemed slightly childish. However, there was nothing childish about the refreshments, the main point of any party, birthday or not.

As soon as the party was over Susan hurried home and burst into the house shouting, "Hey, Mike, how do you feel now?"

"Horrible," he answered, coming to the head of the stairs and standing there, arms hanging way down below the sleeves of his too small bathrobe.

He looked so discouraged Susan said, "You'd feel great if I told you something I know and you don't." Of course he wanted to know what it was and how come she knew and he didn't. And she told him, "I know because I'm a magician and I can't tell because I promised not to. I'll give a hint, though. It has to do with you and Pete Griffith's accident. That's all I should say, any more might give it away. Hugo will tell you the rest soon."

The hint had a healing effect. Mike began to feel better right away and by morning his temperature was normal.

Around ten o'clock, while Susan was cleaning her room (Mother said she couldn't go to the shop until it was in perfect order), the telephone rang. She dropped the dust cloth and ran to answer it. It was Hugo wanting to speak to Mike who trailed down the steps, bedroom slippers slapping, bathrobe belt dragging like a cat's long tail.

Susan hung around the living room door, listening. From Mike's end of the conversation she was pretty sure Hugo was telling him the news. Twice he let out jubilant yelps. Then, after listening a long time, nodding his head, scratching his knee, he exclaimed, "The game called off! Seven guys sick!"

"Let me speak to Hugo, please," Susan said, pulling at her brother's sleeve. "I want to ask him something."

Ignoring her, Mike talked on and on about football until Susan thought she'd collapse on the rug from waiting. Finally he said, "Before you hang up, Hugo, my sister wants to ask you something. How should I know what? Hold on, here she is."

Susan grabbed the phone. "Good morning, Hugo. How is Trunko? That's good. Sereena's fine, too, and Mike is much better. What I wanted to ask is, since the game's been called off, how about helping Mrs. Gaffney and me move furniture and things down at *The Cat's Place*? Yes, that's the new name for the shop, named after you know who. You can't? Well, later on maybe you and Mike can both help. Bye."

She hung up the receiver and right away the telephone rang again. This time it was Joyce Gibbs and she did practically every bit of the talking. All Susan said was, "He did? *That* much? Are you sure?"

As soon as Susan hung up, she faced Mother and Mike who were listening on the landing and said, her eyes sending off sparks, "Guess what? Joyce says the appraiser says, and he knows because he works at the Baltimore Museum and really knows about things like dollhouses, that mine is worth a *thousand dollars.*"

"Yours!" Mother said. "What do you mean yours? I thought the dollhouse was Mrs. Gaffney's."

"It was. But she sold it to me."

"For how much and where did you get the money to pay for it?" Mother asked as she came down the steps, her face a knot of worry.

"I haven't paid for it yet, Mother," was the answer. "I'm going to work it off, helping at the shop, the way I worked off most of the broken teapot debt. Mrs. Gaffney said I could have the house for twenty-five dollars, and the furniture and dolls for ten more."

"Wow," Mike said. "A thousand dollars worth for thirty-five. Not bad."

Susan, pleased as could be, admitted that she'd made a real bargain. Mother was not pleased. "There may be a legal question involved," she said, frowning thoughtfully. "If Mrs. Gaffney did not know the value of the dollhouse, and apparently she didn't, the deal may not be valid. Was the agreement to pay written down, Susan?"

"No, we just talked it. With Mrs. Gaffney that's as good as written down. She'd never go back on her word."

"Considering so much money is at stake, I trust you won't

hold her to it," Mother said and Susan was quick to ask, "What do you mean, not hold her to it? The dollhouse is mine and that is all settled."

"I know, I know, Susan," Mother said. "I'm not telling you what to do, merely suggesting that it would be gracious of you to step down and let Mrs. Gaffney keep or sell the valuable dollhouse as she chooses. That's all."

"I see," Susan said. "Well, I'm sorry to disappoint you, Mother. What's mine is mine and that is all there is to it. If you'd come with me to see it, you'd know how I feel about it. Come now, I want you to see it. Please, Mother. It won't take long. You can run both ways."

"Another time, dear, I'm up-to-my-neck busy today."

"Now," Susan begged.

Mother gave in, saying, "You win." She raised her voice to her son who had gone upstairs, "Keep an eye on the soup, Mike. I'm going down to Gaffney's for a quick look at the famous dollhouse."

"*The Cat's Place,*" Susan corrected her as they went out the door.

"*The Cat's Place,*" repeated Mother.

The two of them walked briskly down the hill and on down the road. Mrs. Gaffney must have seen them coming, for she opened the upstairs window, stuck her head out, and called cheerfully, "Good morning, Mrs. Prescott, you too, Susan. Here is the key."

She tossed it to them, saying, "Go on in and make your-selves at home. Sereena and I overslept this morning. We'll be down shortly."

Susan picked up the key, a large, old-timey one, unlocked the door, and led the way to the dollhouse.

Mother loved it on sight. She sat on the floor in front of it, Susan close beside her, and didn't miss a thing, not even the pots and pans in the tiny kitchen cupboard.

"It is choice, Susan," she said. "Simply choice. No wonder the appraiser is enthusiastic about it. Anybody would be."

Picking up the purple velvet stuffed living room chair, she said, "This is not a toy. It belongs in a museum. The whole house and everything in it does." She put down the chair and reached for the father doll, Susan saying proudly, "That's Mr. Charles Ravenell Barr. Isn't he marvelous? And don't miss the baby."

Mother looked with delight at the baby asleep in its crib, then she got to her feet, saying, "I must go. It is easy to see why you wouldn't want to give up such a treasure, dear. Even so—well, enough for now. I don't want to spoil your fun. Tell Mrs. Gaffney I'm sorry not to have a visit with her, maybe next time."

She didn't say a word about not seeing Sereena. Watching Mother go out the door, Susan wondered how anybody could be so nice in all ways except one.

Now for the sign. Susan found a board standing behind

the kitchen stove, warped a little and too long. But it would do. "Any saw around here?" she called out in a loud voice.

Coming downstairs, Mrs. Gaffney answered, "On the blanket chest in my room. I was trying to level a chair yesterday and forgot to bring it down. Your mother gone already? I wanted to hear what she had to say about your dollhouse."

"She was sorry not to see you, but she had to go. She's wild about the dollhouse—almost as wild about it as I am, though in a different way. Her way. I'll get the saw now."

Susan brushed past Mrs. Gaffney and ran up the steps lightly, her feet barely touching the worn treds. She went into Mrs. Gaffney's bedroom, the right-hand room at the top of the landing. What a dismal sight it was, the opposite of her own pretty pink room. The wallpaper was peeling off and brown spots on the ceiling showed where rain had leaked through. The unmade bed sagged and the drab, thrown-back army blanket exposed rumpled, dull sheets.

The bed was not all dull. In the middle Sereena was sleeping peacefully. Susan swooped her up in her arms and hugged her. Then she picked up the saw and went downstairs again, not easy to do with cat in one arm and saw in the other. If Sereena hadn't held on tightly, Susan would never have made it. Cats are good at holding on.

Susan spilled Sereena on the red sofa, took the saw out into the kitchen, and set to work sawing off the end of the board. Mrs. Gaffney stood by, eating an orange and giving advice. "Don't push so hard, pull it easy, easy. That's better."

Finally after much jamming, starting, stopping, resting, and going back to work, the end of the board dropped to the floor. "Now we need some sandpaper," Susan said, feeling the rough edge with her hand.

As Mrs. Gaffney didn't have any, Susan said she'd go home and get some. At the door she stopped, turned around, and said, "Did Joyce tell you my dollhouse is worth a fortune?" and Mrs. Gaffney replied, "No, but the appraiser did. He said the Museum would like to buy it for the Children's Wing."

"The Museum? Really? That counts for a lot, doesn't it?"

"It certainly does," declared Mrs. Gaffney; then wistfully she added, "I've never had anything of mine bought by a museum. The appraiser said the four-poster bed alone was worth two hundred dollars."

The old woman shook her head and examined her fingernails closely before saying, "What I couldn't do with a thousand dollars." She looked straight at Susan. "He offered me that much and I have a notion he'd go higher if pressed."

"You told him it was mine, didn't you?" asked Susan, and she felt uneasy until Mrs. Gaffney said, "Yes—I told him it had already been sold."

"I'm glad you did," Susan was quick to say. "I wouldn't want anybody, not even Joyce Gibbs, to get hopes up for nothing and I certainly wouldn't want the Museum to. I'll go now for the sandpaper, be right back."

"Take your time," Mrs. Gaffney said with a deep sigh.

Susan left the antique shop in a sober mood and walked toward home slowly, head bent down, thinking. If only she had a magic wand like other magicians had, she'd wave it right now and *pouff* everything would be splendid for Mrs. Gaffney—shop roof mended, floors fixed, building painted inside and out. Mrs. Gaffney herself would be done over too. With a new hairdo, new dress, new shoes, new sweater, new tooth, she'd be a stylish witch instead of the other kind.

Well, Susan didn't have a wand and wishing wasn't strong enough. She couldn't give up the dollhouse so Mrs. Gaffney could pocket the fortune—she wanted it too much. She was a hard worker, though. If she tended to things one by one, eventually they'd get done. Making *The Cat's Place* sign was a starter. She'd fetch the sandpaper, hurry back to the shop, and finish the job.

15

A Magic Wand

WHEN SUSAN reached the gate she saw Mike standing on the front porch, a blanket wrapped around his shoulders.

"Hurry up," he called to her in an irritated tone of voice. "What's the big idea you walking so blasted slow?"

She stepped faster along the path, yanking up her jeans and stuffing in her shirt tail. "I was thinking about important things, Mike. What's up?"

"Plenty." He waited until she was on the step close to him before he said, lowering his voice to almost a whisper, "Dad's here."

Typical, Susan thought to herself, gritting her teeth. When you expected him, waited for him, he didn't come. When you didn't expect him, he came. She pushed her brother aside, hurried into the house, crossed the hall and looked through the living room door. There was Dad, dark, stocky, sitting in his chair by the window, reading the paper as though he'd never gone away.

"Hello, Babe," he said as he got to his feet, the paper sliding to the floor. He held out his arms to her, smiling a warm smile with that attractive mouth of his.

Cat, Mrs. Gaffney, dollhouse, everything vanished from Susan's thoughts. Nothing was left except Dad. Susan wanted to throw herself on him, hug him madly, weep, beg him not to go away again, to stay forever, the way she did the last time he came home.

Instead, she held up her cheek to be kissed, saying, "Hello, Dad. It's nice to see you. How long will you be with us this time?" And she didn't bat an eye when he answered, "My plane leaves at two forty-five. I planned to take the six fifteen but when I found the football game had been called off I phoned the airport and changed my reservation."

"I see," Susan said, and for the first time she almost did. "Come next week or the week after or most any Saturday. Mike will be playing practically every game from now on. He's first string."

"So I hear. I'm glad he finally made it."

"Me, too," Susan said, swinging her left foot in the air as high as it would go for something to do.

Dad sat down again and pulled the desk chair over closer to him, saying, "Sit down, Babe, and bring me up to date on news about you."

"Well," Susan said, sitting bolt upright on the edge of the chair, facing her father, "First and most important is my cat, Sereena. She stays down at what used to be Gaffney's Antiques shop. It's called *The Cat's Place* now, named after Sereena. You know the shop, Dad, the little spooky one down on Falls Road. I'm helping Mrs. Gaffney fix it up so it won't always be spooky."

She folded her hands. "Anyway, cats like spooky places and spooky people. At least Sereena does. She stays at the shop because she wants to, because cats are not allowed on Bird Lane, and for another reason . . ."

She wouldn't let herself say one word against Mother. "Want to meet Sereena and Mrs. Gaffney, Dad? We'll have time before lunch if we go fast."

Dad said he'd take a rain check, meet them next time he came. Right then Mother appeared in the doorway and announced that lunch was ready, would Susan wash her hands quickly and call Mike.

Susan went into the hall, turned around at the door and said to her father, "I'll tell you the rest about me some day when we have plenty of time. It's a long story that started with Trunko, the white elephant. If it weren't for Trunko there might never have been Sereena. Of course she'd have been a cat somewhere, but not mine."

"Hurry, Susan," Mother called from the kitchen, "I'm dishing up."

Susan flew up the steps, shouting, "Mike, lunch is ready." Two minutes later she was back downstairs sitting in her chair at the dining room table on Dad's right, across from Mike.

Everything was so good—Mother's homemade vegetable soup, the best anywhere, hot biscuits, and Mrs. Benson's apple jelly. Not the conversation, though. It was stiff and formal, with everybody trying too hard to make things seem as though the family was together in one piece the way it used to be—and wasn't anymore.

Susan was glad when the meal was over. Truthfully, in spite of how much she loved him, she was glad when Dad left too.

From the living room window she watched him walk down the path and step into a taxi waiting there for him. As the taxi went out of sight down the lane, a new kind of feeling engulfed Susan—not fanciful but solid earth real. The magic part of living was how you fit yourself around real things, she guessed. A magician was extra good at fitting. That's why being one was important.

Dad was not ever coming home to stay because he'd fitted himself around somebody else, someplace else. He'd always come and go. When he came she'd be glad to see him and when he left, like just now, she'd open her hands, spread her fingers, and let him go.

She held out both hands and spread her fingers as wide

as she could. Yes. From now on things were going to be all right. Well, not all right, standable was more like it.

Hearing the rattle of dishes Susan went into the kitchen where Mother was rinsing off the soup plates, or had been. Right then she was blowing her nose, using one of Dad's worn-out handkerchiefs, and her eyes were red.

"I must have picked up Mike's bug," she said. Susan knew better. She'd been weeping and didn't want anybody to know.

Susan, pretending she didn't know, handed her Mother a tea towel saying, "I'll wash. You wipe and listen. I want to tell you the latest dollhouse news. As co-owner you should be up to date.

"Co-owner?"

"Yes, it's going to be ours, yours and mine the way Trunko was."

"I'm proud to be included," Mother said. "And I'd be very proud to have the dollhouse in our house if circumstances were different. As things are, though, I'd—"

Susan interrupted, hand raised in a stop traffic gesture. "Wait. I know what you were about to say and I don't want to hear it. Please, Mother. Okay?"

"Okay." Mother didn't like the word okay one bit but occasionally she let herself use it. "Get on with the dishes, dear. At this rate we'll never get out of the kitchen."

Not the neatest dishwasher in the world, Susan slopped soapy water down her front and on the floor while attacking the first soup bowl. She mopped up swiftly, tied the red checked apron around her waist, and tackled the job again.

Washing away happily, she told Mother about the Museum wanting the dollhouse for the Children's Wing. She said she bet anything Joyce Gibbs would want it more now than ever. She herself would a whole lot rather see the Museum have it than Joyce, though of course neither of them would ever get it.

When she paused long enough to take a big breath, Mother said, "The Museum is the perfect place for the dollhouse—there in the children's room where everybody can enjoy it."

"I knew you were going to say that, Mother. I just knew it."

Mother went on, "At the Museum it would belong to *all* of the children of Baltimore."

"Including Joyce Gibbs, I presume," stated Susan reluctantly.

And Mother said, "Including Joyce Gibbs and Susan Prescott."

"Never," Susan said and she changed the subject to Mrs. Gaffney, telling Mother what a mess her bedroom was, how everything in the shop was falling to pieces, floor, roof, everything, and how she'd give anything if she had a magic wand to wave and change things with a *pouff*.

"You have a magic wand," Mother said as she reached high to put the plates on the top shelf of the cupboard over the sink.

"What do you mean?"

"The dollhouse could be a magic wand."

"The dollhouse?"

Mother nodded. "Think about it, Susan, and you'll know it could be."

Susan smoothed down the damp apron with both hands and closed her eyes to let silver darts of thought shoot through her head.

Suddenly she opened her eyes and leaped into the air, knocking the soup kettle off of the drain. "A wand it is, Mother!" she exclaimed, "and that is not all. I *want* to give it up more than I want to keep it. All at once I really do."

"Are you sure?" Mother asked, not sure herself now that Susan had changed her mind. "You've lost so much already — your father, the white elephant, the cat."

"I am sure," declared Susan, arms folded across her wet chest. "Anyway, magicians don't lose. They win. Dad, Trunko, and Sereena are mine still in a way." She looked up at her mother. "And you are mine in all ways for always."

Mother gave her a rare, tight hug and Mike, coming into the kitchen for one more biscuit, said, "What about me?"

"You, too, Mike. Everybody knows a brother is for always."

Susan's mood changed and she said, "About the doll-house. I'll go down to the shop right now and tell Mrs. Gaffney it is hers. Any sandpaper around here? I need some for the new *Cat's Place* sign I'm making."

Mike found sandpaper in the cellar, three grades—fine, medium, and coarse. Susan took a sheet of each variety and started toward the door. Before going out she said, "To celebrate the magic wand, let's play gin rummy again tonight, Mother. We had so much fun last time. Mike can play with us if he wants to."

Mother said fine, she'd set the stage for a big evening, card table up, cards shuffled ready to deal as soon as Susan got home. And she'd bake brownies right now to add the final touch. Mike said to count him out, he wasn't going to risk getting clobbered by a pair of card sharks, and besides Hugo was coming over after supper.

Susan left the house and walked down Bird Lane in high gear. Just wait until Joyce Gibbs heard the latest news and found out what kind of a girl Susan Prescott had turned out to be, was turning out to be, rather. Susan was far from finished.

In front of *The Cat's Place* she stopped, shut her eyes, crossed her fingers, and saw by magic the brilliant blue, star-dotted future of a witch, a magic salescat, and a magician.

Back to the real world again, she opened the shop door and went in.